1981

Sr. Miriam Clare

The Nature
of Literature

The Nature of Literature

WRITING ON LITERARY TOPICS

WILLIAM F. IRMSCHER
University of Washington

HOLT, RINEHART AND WINSTON, INC.

New York Chicago San Francisco Atlanta Dallas
Montreal Toronto

Library of Congress Cataloging in Publication Data

Irmscher, William F.
  The nature of literature.

  Includes index.
  1. Criticism. 2. Rhetoric. I. Title.
PN81.I7   801'.95   74–22085

ISBN: 0–03–013286–X

5 6 7 8 9   059   9 8 7 6 5 4 3 2 1

Acknowledgments

Excerpt from *The American Dream* by Edward Albee, reprinted by permission of Coward, McCann & Geoghegan, Inc. Copyright © 1960, 1961 by Edward Albee.

"my sweet old etcetera" by E. E. Cummings. Copyright 1926 by Horace Liveright, 1954 by E. E. Cummings. Reprinted from *Complete Poems 1913–1962* by E. E. Cummings by permission of Harcourt Brace Jovanovich, Inc.

Excerpts from *Murder in the Cathedral* by T. S. Eliot, reprinted by permission of Harcourt Brace Jovanovich, Inc., and Faber and Faber, Ltd.

"Dust of Snow" and excerpt from "Mending Wall" by Robert Frost. From *The Poetry of Robert Frost* edited by Edward Connery Lathem. Copyright 1923, 1930, 1939, © 1969 by Holt, Rinehart and Winston, Inc. Copyright 1951, © 1958 by Robert Frost. Copyright © 1967 by Lesley Frost Ballantine. Reprinted by permission of Holt, Rinehart and Winston, Inc.

Excerpt from "The Windhover" by Gerard Manley Hopkins. From *Poems of Gerard Manley Hopkins* by Gerard Manley Hopkins, reprinted by permission of Oxford University Press.

Excerpt from "Reveille" from "A Shropshire Lad"; Authorized Edition, from *The Collected Poems of A. E. Housman.* Copyright 1939, 1940 ©

1965 by Holt, Rinehart and Winston, Inc. Copyright © 1967, 1968 by Robert E. Symons. Reprinted by permission of Holt, Rinehart and Winston, Inc.; The Society of Authors as the literary representative of the Estate of A. E. Housman; and Jonathan Cape Ltd., Publishers of A. E. Housman's *Collected Poems.*

Excerpt from *The Bald Soprano* by Eugene Ionesco. Copyright © 1965 by Grove Press, Inc.; excerpt from "The Lesson" from *Four Plays* by Eugene Ionesco. Copyright © 1958 by Grove Press, Inc.; excerpt from *Exit the King* by Eugene Ionesco. Copyright © 1963 by John Calder, Ltd. Reprinted by permission of Grove Press, Inc.

"The Death of the Ball Turret Gunner" by Randall Jarrell. Reprinted with the permission of Farrar, Straus & Giroux, Inc., from *The Complete Poems* by Randall Jarrell, copyright © 1945, 1969 by Mrs. Randall Jarrell.

Excerpt from "Boots" by Rudyard Kipling. From *Kipling: A Selection of His Stories and Poems* by Rudyard Kipling. Reprinted by permission of Doubleday & Company, Inc., and Mrs. George Bambridge and the Macmillan Company of Canada.

Excerpt from "Come Live with Me and Be My Love" by C. Day Lewis. From *Collected Poems (1954)* by C. Day Lewis, copyright 1954 by C. Day Lewis. Reprinted by permission of the Harold Matson Company, Inc.

"The End of the World" by Archibald MacLeish. From *Collected Poems, 1917–1952* by Archibald MacLeish, copyright © 1962 by Archibald MacLeish. Reprinted by permission of Houghton Mifflin Company.

Excerpt from "Portrait of the Artist As a Prematurely Old Man" by Ogden Nash. From *Verses from 1929 On* by Ogden Nash, by permission of Little, Brown and Co. Copyright 1934 by The Curtis Publishing Co.

"Revolution: The Vicious Circle" by John Nist. From *College Composition and Communication.* Copyright © 1968 by the National Council of Teachers of English. Reprinted by permission of the publisher and the author.

Excerpt from "Arms and the Boy" by Wilfred Owen. From Wilfred Owen, *Collected Poems.* Copyright Chatto & Windus, Ltd., 1946 © 1963. Reprinted by permission of New Directions Publishing Corporation, the Executors of the Estate of Harold Owen, and Chatto & Windus, Ltd.

Excerpt from "Dance Figure" by Ezra Pound. From Ezra Pound, *Personae.* Copyright 1926 by Ezra Pound. Reprinted by permission of New Directions Publishing Corporation.

Excerpt from "Winter Remembered" by John Crowe Ransom. From *Selected Poems,* Third Edition, Revised and Enlarged, by John Crowe Ransom, copyright 1927 by Alfred A. Knopf, Inc., and renewed 1955 by John Crowe Ransom. Reprinted by permission of Alfred A. Knopf, Inc.

"Luke Havergal" by Edwin Arlington Robinson is reprinted by permission of Charles Scribner's Sons from *The Children of the Night* by Edwin Arlington Robinson.

Excerpt from *Man and Superman* by George Bernard Shaw. Reprinted by permission of The Society of Authors on behalf of the Bernard Shaw Estate.

Excerpt from "Aubade" by Edith Sitwell. From *Collected Poems of Edith Sitwell*. Reprinted by permission of Vanguard Press, Inc., and David Higham Associates, Ltd.

"Anecdote of the Jar" by Wallace Stevens. Copyright 1923 and renewed 1951 by Wallace Stevens. Reprinted from *The Collected Poems of Wallace Stevens* by permission of Alfred A. Knopf, Inc.

Excerpts from "And Death Shall Have No Dominion" and "Do Not Go Gentle Into That Good Night" by Dylan Thomas. From *The Poems of Dylan Thomas*. Copyright 1946 by New Directions Publishing Corporation, 1952 by Dylan Thomas. Reprinted by permission of New Directions Publishing Corporation. From *Collected Poems* by Dylan Thomas. Reprinted by permission of J. M. Dent & Sons, Ltd., and the Trustees for the Copyrights of the late Dylan Thomas.

Excerpt from *Man and the Masses* by Ernst Toller. Reprinted by permission of Sidney Kaufman on behalf of the Ernst Toller Estate.

Excerpt from *The Glass Menagerie* by Tennessee Williams, Copyright 1945 by Tennessee Williams and Edwina D. Williams. Reprinted by permission of Random House, Inc.

Preface

To say the least, the subject of this book on literature is vast. And I hardly need to add the obvious point that hundreds of volumes could be written about literature to join the thousands that have already been written. But for writing purposes volumes are not needed, perhaps only a slim volume. Effectiveness does not depend on exhaustiveness. Thus I have aimed for brevity, but also for completeness and readability—high ambitions, I realize.

This book treats literature in terms of seven major components —character, action, setting, form, language, style, and meaning. Nevertheless, instructors need not organize their courses accordingly in order to use it. If students read the book in its entirety at the beginning of the course, instructors are free to proceed as they like. Students, however, have the overview and the fundamentals they need, and they always have the option of returning to those sections that provide practical aids to get the process of composition moving and of using the Glossary for reference. This book is intended as a catalyst to be added to a course, not a recipe book to be followed step by step.

The college student who may have read quite a bit throughout his high school years has seldom had the opportunity to assume an overview. Poems, plays, and stories have followed one after the other. They are all literature, of course. But what is literature? What do the genres have in common? How do they differ from one another? In what terms do we come to grips with their implications? These are the kinds of questions this book is intended to answer.

I realize that many literature classes and writing classes that include literature treat three major genres, each in turn. A three-part division would seem a logical organization for a book of this kind—three genres, treated separately: fiction, then drama, then poetry. I am also aware that each of the genres invites a predominant emphasis, such as point of view in fiction, character in drama, or the persona in poetry. A three-part treatment might emphasize that point to a greater extent. But the "most logical" and familiar organization is not always the most effective, particularly if we are interested in encouraging inventiveness in writing about literature. Without doubt, students need directions, but we do not always have to provide them with clearly marked maps indicating the well-paved highways. I have found that students, knowing where they are expected to go, can discover some remarkably fascinating routes. This book is designed to help·them, not by limiting them, but by opening up new possibilities.

• • •

In the preparation of this manuscript, I have been particularly indebted to Mrs. Pamela Forcey of Holt, Rinehart and Winston for her editorial assistance. As always, I am grateful for the incomparable efficiency and cooperation of my secretary, Mrs. Shirley Hanson.

W. F. I.

Contents

3

Action 35

4

Setting 45

5

Form and Structure 52

6
Language, Symbol, and Imagery   67

7
Stylistic Effects   85

8
Thought and Meaning   94

9
Writing on Literary Topics 107

The Nature of Literature

1

The Nature
of Literature

What Literary Criticism Is and Is Not

We all tend by nature to be critics. This does not mean that we want to find fault with things. What it does mean is that we want to ask questions, try to understand, and come to conclusions about things we like or do not like. In other words, we respond. We respond, either consciously or subconsciously, every time we hear a speech, see a film, or listen to a concert. We respond in the same way when we read. Literary criticism is simply a type of response to reading. Yet when we suddenly introduce the rather formidable term "literary criticism," we seem to remove reading from common experience and turn it into a specialized process. Actually, the opposite is true: literary criticism enables us to bring what we read into our own personal experience and thus to respond to it fully and completely. This complete response can sometimes awaken strong feelings within us and lead us to insights about experience that are totally revealing.

But we do not necessarily become instant experts in literary criticism because we are capable of responding. It is also a skill that requires knowledge and practice. And, as with most other skills, some people are consistently better at it than others. They may know more, they may have had an earlier start, they may practice more, they may be more sensitive to subtleties, they may simply be more observant. The important point, however, is that those who are really interested can work to overcome their limitations and develop this skill. Helping you become a better reader and critic is the purpose of this book.

What further is literary criticism? In simplest terms, it is an orderly way of looking at a literary work—asking questions about it—what has been called "discovery of design." It might also be called "discovery *by* design." For criticism is discovery. It is not a deathblow to the literary work. It is not necessarily a negative judgment. Criticism can be both positive and negative. It is not necessarily a tearing apart, a way of spoiling enjoyment. It is actually a way of enhancing enjoyment. It is most meaningful when it provides a fresh way of seeing—a new view and a new kind of understanding.

Criticism, then, can be thought of as a kind of exploring, probing, playing with possibilities, gambling and usually winning, if only a little. It always demands thought and involvement. It does not always have to be strictly writing *about* literature; it can also be personal expression. It can be writing *through* literature, *with* literature, *by means of* literature, and always, one hopes, *for* literature.

The Meaning of Literature

Literature is an art expressed in words. Thus, it is not dance; it is not music; it is not cinematography. It may have elements in common with each of these other arts, but each art has its own identity and special means of expression. Each must be understood in terms of its own forms, conventions, and effects. Literature as a verbal art must also be understood in its own terms.

Today, we have come to think of literature almost exclusively as written expression, forgetting that much of what we now preserve in written form was once perpetuated by an oral tradition. Literature, of course, may be either written or spoken. As the term has been narrowed in one sense, it has been extended in another. That is, the word "literature" also is frequently used in a very general sense to refer to the whole body of writing in a culture, regardless of its purpose. In this sense, both informative writing and imaginative writing clearly belong to our literature. In a restricted sense, however, literature has come to be identified particularly with artistic forms of verbal expression, especially fiction, drama, poetry, and kinds of prose that reveal an imaginative mind at work—some familiar essays, biographies, autobiographies, and letters. All of these may be differentiated from prose that is designed primarily for explanation and persuasion—what we commonly call expository prose. Thus, not much journalistic prose, for example, has gained literary status, and seldom does technical, scholarly, and, alas, textbook writing achieve such status. Nevertheless, the distinction between imaginative and expository writing is not necessarily based on quality, but on purpose and method.

How do these purposes and methods vary? Let us take one topic as an example—the kind of injustice that can occur in the exercise of the law, particularly in the courts. Is there such a thing as an appeal to a higher justice beyond the laws that men make and judges enforce? Suppose a writer takes the position that civil law as he observes it is not in harmony with what he thinks is a higher order of justice, what we rather abstractly call natural law or moral law. How can this distinction be made clear?

Presumably one way a writer can make the distinction clear is to write an essay that tries to define terms. He can attempt to define "moral law" and state what its source is and how it operates. Then, if moral law and civil law conflict with one another, he can weigh the claims of each. He can try to explain and illustrate, proceeding by fairly standard kinds of reasoning, drawing out the thought and trying to make the abstractions as concrete as possible. But the difficulties of this approach are apparent even in this somewhat brief description of it. Abstractions are difficult to grasp.

A writer has an alternative, however. Instead of dealing directly with ideas, he can attempt to represent them indirectly by creating a fictional world. Typically, this is the way of the storyteller, dramatist, and poet. This is the way Herman Melville treats the conflict between civil law and moral law in his story *Billy Budd*. Up to this point, the issue we have been discussing may seem a bit difficult to penetrate, so let us see how Melville makes it clear through narrative and actually causes us to take the side of one law against the other.

The main character of Melville's story *Billy Budd* is a youthful seaman, an almost unnaturally naive and innocent young man. We seldom meet people like Billy, but we would like to believe they exist. Or perhaps we would like to believe we have an element of Billy's innocence in our own nature. At any rate, we like him. We do not want to see him unnecessarily harmed. Yet, in the course of this story, we see him falsely and helplessly accused of plotting mutiny by a strangely diabolical figure named Claggert, whom we instinctively dislike. In a climactic confrontation between Billy and Claggert, Billy in anger strikes Claggert with his fist and kills him. All of the circumstances outlined in the story are against Billy. The military court is obligated to call the act murder under the dictates of military law governing a ship in time of war. Yet, as much as we know that the law has been impartially applied, we also know that even as Billy hangs upon the gibbet the sentence against him has been cruel and unjust, that a higher law exonerates him.

Does one know precisely what this higher moral law is after having read *Billy Budd*? Perhaps not. Melville's story certainly gives us little rational justification for belief in a higher justice, but, without doubt, it gives us a strong moral conviction that such a force operates in our thinking and influences our decisions. Melville makes us first feel a position, then reflect upon it. He presents a paradox of innocence and guilt strangely reversed. Billy is sentenced to die by the decision of the military court, and we are left to accede to the practical and pitiless claims of human law if we also believe that every man cannot be his own law. But Melville also lets us know that Billy is innocent. For the short span of time that we read the story, Melville creates a world for us that we cannot change. It is a world in which the central issue of justice is dramatized by characters who involve us not only in their own dilemma but in the total continuing human dilemma of which we are all a part.

Who will say that literature of this kind is incapable of explaining or promoting belief or even of moving people to action?

The Fictional Universe

Characteristically, literature acts through a world of its own; it creates its own fictional universe. It may be as completely fanciful as the setting of *Alice's Adventures in Wonderland* or as graphic as scenes in *Crime and Punishment*. Perhaps one of the greatest obstacles to understanding literature is to assume that the literary work, even when it seems most factual, is an actual transcription of real life. No matter how faithfully a writer holds to experience, what he writes is only an approximation of actuality. We read only a digest, a selection of details from the multitude of words and gestures and actions that are a part of everyday living. In the universe of fiction, we encounter only segments and scenes of the lives of characters. Almost all of the repetitious details of everyday living are taken for granted—bathing, taking out the garbage, washing the car, going to the supermarket, writing the monthly checks. These may be included only if they provide the writer an occasion to reveal something of significance about a character; otherwise, they are simply omitted in the abbreviated world of fiction. The world of fiction has an existence independent of anything else. It does not need to correspond to what we see about us. It is not justified by saying that it is very much like the world we know. In fact, though fiction may at times be grotesque, it is more often less strange than truth. It has to be. If a writer included in a story the kinds of incredible accidents and deaths we read about in the daily newspaper, he would be accused of cheap sensationalism. In creating an illusion of reality, a writer is first bound to what is probable, not what is possible.

Even though the fictional universe customarily observes natural law and circumstance, it is not necessarily held to it as the real world is. When the ancient storyteller chooses to have the goddess Artemis seize Iphigenia from the sacrificial altar and carry her off in a cloud to a distant land, he has introduced a miraculous event that dramatizes his concern for the innocence of Iphigenia. He would have us believe that there is a force which preserves good in the world. It is his viewpoint, not universally accepted to be sure, but one that many people believe. The narration of the ancient myth, therefore, may not correspond to the external system of logic and law in nature we subscribe to, but it does correspond to an inner psychic system within those who choose to believe in a moral and purposive universe. The rescue of Iphigenia is an objectification of a way of feeling and believing which is not less true because it is improbable; it may be less true literally, to be sure, but not less true metaphorically. We need only remind ourselves that Superman is a modern mythological figure who serves the same purpose. He arrives always in the nick of time to save the innocent and foil the forces of evil. He also is a fictional objectification of basic beliefs that are common in our society.

Misconceptions about the fictional universe may account for the fact that some readers are actually alienated by what they find in literature. They do not see what they hope to see; they do not find out what they want to find out. The world of a literary work is incomplete. We do not know how Hamlet spent his days at Heidelberg University, if that concerns anyone. A literary work operates on its own assumptions; Humpty Dumpty's famous statement to Alice "When *I* use a word, it means just what I choose it to mean—neither more nor less," is sometimes more true of literature than we would like it to be. A literary work functions by its own internal laws; it observes its own conventions; it promotes its own values. All of these may be different from what we are familiar with. They require us to suspend our own beliefs to accept others' beliefs. The world we experience in a novel or play may be a world that an author thinks ought to be, not what is. It may be a world that he imaginatively creates to move readers beyond the narrow limits of their own thinking and experience. Yet, for all of the unfamiliarities we may encounter in the world of a literary work, we know from the vast literature that has been written that most works touch on human experience, even when they are merely helping us escape the harshness of everyday living. We know also that literature is capable of transcending time and place. *Gulliver's Travels* is not irrelevant because it was written in the eighteenth century. It is still readable and meaningful because it embodies a host of universal truths.

In a play by Oscar Wilde, one of the characters says, "Life imitates Art far more than Art imitates Life." The statement reverses what many people may think about literature. But if that statement is essentially true, then we do not need to use experience as a measuring stick for literature. We may learn from it. In fact, it may well set the measures for us.

The Influence of Literature

What is literature capable of doing? What means does it use to affect the reader? An attempt to answer these questions directly forces us to see that literature shares many elements in common with other art forms, even though the total effect of each may be different; but that, finally, literature is distinct from dance or painting or music in the particular effects it can create.

How, then, does literature function and with what effects?

1. Through *character*, literature reveals human motives; it invites identification and reaction.
2. Through *actions and situations*, literature brings characters into relationships with one another or into relationships with institutions and forces beyond their control; it reveals man in conflict.
3. Through its own *compressed world*, it focuses on its central concern without being distracted by other details of life; it sorts out and orders the experiences of its characters; it objectifies experience so that it can be viewed as a whole and reflected on; it shields the reader from the intensity of actual experiences.
4. Through *form*, it orders the action, shapes the thought, and channels the feeling.
5. Through *language, symbol, and imagery*, it creates effects of beauty and ugliness; it stimulates the imagination; it moves the audience to respond.
6. Through *style*, it embodies the uniqueness of one writer's way of

looking at things and provides us the pleasure of reading him or her.

7. Through *thought*, it mirrors experience, embodies wisdom, anatomizes the world, raises issues, and searches for solutions.

It should be emphasized here that these are the basic concerns of anyone writing about literature. All that follows in Sections 2–8 is expansion and illustration of these seven major points.

The Genres

Among the various kinds of literary production, three predominate: fiction, drama, and poetry. These are the major literary genres. One might add to the list or subclassify them, but these represent three distinct classes because each depends on its own techniques and effects.

Almost anyone recognizes the differences in appearance between a story, a play, and a poem on the printed page. Yet these differences do not take us very far in differentiating among the three. Ultimately, we begin to use phrases like "dramatic poem" or "poetic prose" or "a reading drama," each of which suggests that the essential qualities of one genre apparently have fused with the essential qualities of another genre. Perhaps a poem has the strong qualities of a drama, or a short story has the effect of a poem, or a drama reads more like a story than a play to be acted.

We are therefore entitled to ask what the essential components of a particular genre are, what characterizes it so that a writer chooses it as opposed to another mode to express himself and why at times he senses the need to fuse the modes. An examination of three skeletal examples of fiction, drama, and poetry may possibly lead us to see more clearly what would be less apparent if we looked at far more complete and sophisticated examples.

The Essential Elements of Fiction

Let us see if we can reduce fiction to its most skeletal form so that we can see the bare bones that underlie its outward form.

First, it might be useful to ask ourselves if we think that any accounting of events, either spoken or written, is fiction. Must we first know whether the events that have occurred are actual or imaginary? For example, is the kind of story a writer tells in an essay for purposes of illustration an example of fiction? Is that kind of anecdote actually an abbreviated version of the form we ordinarily refer to as a short story or novel? In most instances, narrations in any essay are accounts of actual experience, which in the brief space allotted to them depend on compressed action, fragmentary characterization, abbreviated dialogue, and simplified detail to make their point. But making a point is of course the purpose of an illustration, even though as a bonus an anecdote may help an essayist express his thoughts more concretely and even add a bit of pleasure to boot. But the kind of expository narration we are talking about, whether it is actual or imaginary, reduces storytelling to a minimum, giving us only the essentials. Consider this brief example:

> They had lunch together—husband and wife. He ordered drink plentifully, food modestly. She ordered no drink, food plentifully. She soberly attacked her fare, all the while her ear glued to a portable transistor, speechless. He, eyes wandering from her, smiled at me.

This is an account of an actual experience. It has no beginning in a traditional sense; that is, we do not know the circumstances leading up to this moment. It has no outcome; we do not know what eventually happens to this relationship. We are introduced into the middle of a situation that suggests any number of possibilities. A storyteller or novelist might do quite different things with these spare details. He might see the episode only as the beginning of a story that would develop the possibilities of a new relationship suggested by the momentary flirtation in the last sentence. (The word "flirtation" is already an interpretation of the smile.) Or the episode could be seen as an unresolved and undramatic ending of a story about two people whose loveless existence together has been traced in full detail up to this particular moment. Or, in another version, this particular slice-of-life, with a beginning and ending, might be fleshed out by means of dialogue, reminiscence, and interior monologue to tell a story about the conflicts that have brought this marriage to a stage of lifelessness.

A more pragmatic mind, of course, might argue that there is no support for any of these interpretations: that the description represents a passing incident of no significance, that it deals only with superficial details of eating, drinking, listening to the radio, and smiling. The fact that there appears to be an estrangement between the husband and wife could be totally misleading. If we were able to ask her, the wife might explain that her preoccupation with the radio was exceptional, that she had to be away from home and simply did not want to miss the interview of a close friend on a local station. The husband might also explain that his drinking and smiling were quite innocent and unextraordinary.

These diverse ways of looking at the short written experience illustrate an essential difference between fact and fiction. Once the words have been written down, even in the brief form we find here, they have created a fictional universe which is possibly quite different from the actual experiences of the two people who served as the model for the written episode. Thus we must draw a line of distinction between their life-drama in actual experience and the writer's representation of their drama revealed through literature. The difference between life and literature is the way we experience them. The particular circumstances of life or of a novel or of a play may not vary greatly from one another, but the form does. In the nonliterary world, we are our own observers and interpreters. In a story, we are told about the characters; they are permitted to reveal themselves only in part, as opposed to the drama, which depends largely on a technique of self-revelation. In drama, the characters unfold as they speak; we are not told about them. But in either form we are permitted to observe only what the storyteller or dramatist shows us.

If we return to the skeletal example of the story, note that we are told about the husband and wife in a limited way. We have to depend upon a narrator, who in this instance is not an all-knowing author capable of telling us what is going on in the minds of his created characters but someone present in the restaurant who sees two strange people and makes inferences about their lives. Even if the husband and wife were allowed to reveal things about themselves through dialogue in an expanded version, that conversation would have to be overheard by this narrator or spoken directly in his presence or reported to him by another character. If the manner of storytelling were altered altogether, eliminating this narrator, the author himself would be freer to tell us more about the characters. Yet limited narration actually comes closer to the way we learn about other people in experience. We ourselves are creatures of limited perception; we constantly interpret experiences as we see them from our own point of view. Because this is true, we can assume that the way a narrator tells a story can also tell us much about his own character and thinking.

Fiction is characterized chiefly by its manner of narration. In the brief restaurant episode, the narrator selects details. We have no other perspective. In this version, the husband is more sympathetically described than the wife. We would assume that the narrator is a woman, but then we do not have enough story even to know that. If the narrator were a man, the implications of the last sentence would be altered considerably. The incident suggests a possible triangular situation—husband, wife, and rival, but the identity of the rival in this instance could change the nature of the story considerably. It should also not be ignored that the author, the one who writes down the words, is actually an outside agent, a fourth figure working through the narrator. Even from this narrative in miniature, we might infer that this particular writer is not so much interested in the things that happen like eating, drinking, listening to the radio, and smiling as he is in the significance of these events as a commentary upon the marriage. Words like "plentifully," "modestly," "soberly," "speechless," and "wandering" are far more important than the verbs in these few sentences because they set a tone. They influence us to respond to the characters in fairly uniform ways. The method of narration permits the storyteller to be in much more complete control of his effects than the dramatist, who by the restrictions of his form is unable to comment on his characters except as he has them act or speak in particular ways. Both drama and fiction depend on scene, characters, situations, and language, but their form and techniques give each writer different capabilities for literary expression.

Today, fiction is the storyteller's natural medium. Once it was the poem, particularly the epic. Now, however, when a poem tells a story, it is identified as a narrative poem, as if to explain that the poem has borrowed an art not its own. Of the three genres, fiction is the latest to come to full fruition, in the form of the novel, dating from the eighteenth century, and in the short story, dating from the nineteenth. In technique, fiction is perhaps the most expansive and least restricted of the types, allowing the writer great freedom and variety, so that narrative prose can at times create the effects of both drama and poetry. Nevertheless, fiction is basically prose narrative, and if it tends to become more like drama or poetry, we then need to discuss it in terms of those genres.

The Essential Elements of Drama

Just as we have considered the elements that make up fiction and have tried to examine the genre in terms of an elementary form, we can proceed in a similar way with drama. We might ask ourselves whether the following dialogue could possibly be considered a drama in miniature:

The Question Game

No. 1 is on the stage, not doing much of anything. No. 2 enters, apparently confused.

NO. 2   Where am I?
NO. 1   What?
NO. 2   Where am I going?
NO. 1   Where did you come from?

NO. 2   What are you doing here?
NO. 1   Why do you ask?
NO. 2   Who are you, anyway?
NO. 1   What's it to you?
NO. 2   Why are you here?
NO. 1   Me?
NO. 2   Are you mad?
NO. 1   What do you mean?
NO. 2   Are you?
NO. 1   Who do you think you are?
NO. 2   Did God put you here?
NO. 1   What?
NO. 2   Is there a God?
NO. 1   What?
NO. 2   Is there?
NO. 1   How should I know?
NO. 2   Don't you know?
NO. 1   No, of course not. (*Pause*)
NO. 2   Neither do I.

No. 2 exits, leaving No. 1 on the stage, apparently confused.

The first thing we should note is that there are two different sources of information about the setting and the characters: first, in three stage directions, the author gives us a few brief notes about the location (the stage is not actually described) and about the characters ("apparently confused") and about the action (No. 1 present, No. 2 enters, a pause, No. 2 exits, leaving No. 1); then in a series of twenty-one questions and two statements, the un-identified characters reveal things about themselves and about each other. Even though characters in fiction also converse and reveal things about themselves, drama depends almost exclusively on this technique of self-revelation.

Through stage directions, the author also tells us that a change has occurred. At the beginning, No. 2 is "apparently confused"; at the end, No. 1 is also "apparently confused." In the course of the dialogue, we can see how the change occurs. No. 1 is at first "not doing much of anything." No. 2 enters and takes the initiative. His question, "Where am I?" seems to inquire about his location, but, as the dialogue develops, all of No. 2's questions have philosophical overtones. They are inquiries about identity and purpose in life. No. 1, alone and possibly self-confident at first, grows perplexed at the questioning, seems to become irritated, then possibly indignant ("Who do you think you are?"). He makes only one declarative statement ("No, of course not"), which could be interpreted as an admission of agnosticism that he has been forced into. There is a pause; then No. 2 affirms that he doesn't know either. No. 1, in a changed state, is left disturbed.

The characters do not actually say enough for us to be very definite about the content, but there seems to have been a brief conflict, perhaps more internal than external, than a resolution. There seems even to have been some change in both characters as a result of the dialogue. No. 2, only at the end, can affirm something instead of asking a question. No. 1 has had his state of "not doing much of anything" upset. Even though we know nothing about No. 1 and No. 2 as people—what they look like or even whether they are male or female—we know a few of their thoughts and attitudes; and, in these, they have a representativeness.

Nothing much happens in this miniature drama. It cannot be said to have a formal plot. But in a similar way nothing much happens in a play like Samuel Beckett's *Waiting for Godot*. It is a play about waiting. Our brief drama might conceivably be called a play about asking questions, as the title indicates. In its telegraphic style, it is a drama of the dilemma of modern man—his sense of uncertainty. And this skeletal drama does precisely what a far more sophisticated drama does on a larger scale. It reveals a setting in which characters speak, interact, and develop; it comments upon the human scene; it moves us to respond to the thought and emotions expressed. This particular combination of character, action, setting, and thought, using this dialogue form and producing this effect upon an audience, creates a drama.

Is it a good drama? Most likely not. There is actually not enough to tell. The setting is too diffuse, the characters too unearthly, the action too static, the events too limited, the conflict too suppressed, the thought too undeveloped. But it is potential drama. And it should be clear from this skeletal example that not just any conversation produces a drama. Drama develops out of a progression of events, contrasts of character and emotional conflicts, either in action or word. Drama remains even when words are stripped away, even though it then gives up its status as literature. When a play is translated into dance, for example, movement and gesture substitute for words, but the situations and the juxtaposition of characters remain unchanged. Walter Terry once described Herbert Ross's ballet *The Maids*, based upon Genet's play of the same name, as "a superb dance-drama in which attraction and repulsion, desire and abnegation, physical union and individual isolation, and Genet's belief that 'profound unreality' passes itself off 'as reality' are projected through spare and powerful and cuttingly direct choreographic action." His comment suggests that drama lies beneath and behind words and actions, as well as in words and actions.

Drama itself is elemental in its appeal; we use the word "dramatic" to apply to experiences that are lively, striking, intense, and emotionally moving. These are the qualities drama has derived from its theatrical traditions. A student reading drama as literature needs to keep firmly in mind its tradition as a lively art.

The Essential Elements of Poetry

Poetry is yet another form of literary expression, another vehicle of human thought and feeling—perhaps the most misunderstood of the genres because it seems to demand the most of its readers. It is not primarily an acting out of events to be observed; it is not primarily a telling about them; it is something to be experienced itself. It demands not a responding *to*, but a responding *with*. The observer-reader may be frustrated with poetry because he thinks he needs more setting to see, more details to examine, more events to react to. But this reaction comes from failing to realize that the reader often needs to *bring to* the poem more than the poem gives, for this is the way to let the poem act as a catalyst on his imagination and feeling—to let it produce a truly personal experience.

Revolution: The Vicious Circle

JOHN NIST

bread!

b r e a d !

B r e a d !

B r e a d !

B R E A D !

dead-dead-dead-dead-dead-dead-dead-dead-dead-dead-dead.

dead-dead-dead-dead-dead-dead-dead-dead-dead-dead-dead.

dead-dead-dead-dead-dead-dead-dead-dead-dead-dead-dead.

dead-dead-dead-dead-dead-dead-dead-dead-dead-dead-dead.

dead-dead-dead-dead-dead-dead-dead-dead-dead-dead-dead.

bread!

b r e a d !

B r e a d !

B r e a d !

B R E A D !

Because poetry is basically a compressed form of expression, its essentials may be observed in many brief examples. The accompanying poem by John Nist, however, serves as a particularly apt example because it is purged almost completely of dramatic situation, of narrative, of special point of view, and of argument. It permits us to see what other elements work together to produce a poem.

A reader who wants to know exactly what the background or occasion of this poem is or who needs to be given more clues to what the poet himself is trying to say will find little satisfaction in reading it. First, the reader must provide his own setting and characters and actions. The limits to supplying concrete details to this poem are those provided by the title and the two words used in the poem itself. Further, there are no sentences. Nothing is said about "bread;" nothing is said about "dead." Nothing is said explicitly. There are only utterances.

Yet the form of this poem makes a statement. Stanzas 1 and 3 repeat the word "bread" so that there is a visual image of a crescendo of sound. It is almost a cry of basic need; it is a demand unknown people are making of an unknown power structure; it is the voice of revolution in a single word.

The response to that demand is conveyed by a different word— "dead"—in a different pattern. The calm, orderly, row-by-row arrangement suggests the symmetry of crosses on the graves of masses buried together. The poet reading these lines aloud makes them sound like the rat-ta-tat-tat of a machine gun. His reading provides a second interpretation. One is not true, the other false. Both are there. One is a visual image; the other, a sound image.

The third stanza, a repetition of the first, takes the reader back to the subtitle. The cry cannot be stilled by oppressive measures; the cycle continues.

It should be noted that an interpretation of this poem results in translating it into a story, a situation, a drama. It should also be noted that the interpretation is not the poem itself. The poem is a combination of form, image, sound, and rhythm to which the reader is able to respond. It employs rhyme, repetition, and contrast. It appeals both to the eye and to the ear and also to the intellect indirectly through the imagination. The significance of it is not what it says; it is what it does. If the poem is paraphrased, one might conclude that it says very little or that it echoes only a truism. But paraphrasing is not experiencing the poem—the way it expresses the tensions of suffering. Even though this may be a poem about revolution and conflict, the poem itself promotes harmony, identification and understanding among those who read it.

Poetry, more completely than the other forms of literary expression, has the capacity to move from the world of outward circumstance to the inner world of feeling. For that reason, it depends more exclusively than the other genres upon the particularity of the word and the image to evoke feeling. Poetry as a genre does not have to have character, setting, action, and ideas, but it cannot sacrifice rhythm, pattern, image, and sound without losing its identification as poetry. These are its trademarks.

The Changing Genres

To think of genres as rigid categories is to ignore the fact that extremely different works may be quite arbitrarily classified within the same genre. Further, the genres are by no means fixed. Writers reinterpret them so that we are constantly obliged to reassess our preconceptions. Readers who are not willing to do that are not much disposed to accept what experimental writers often attempt to do. When the stage director of a recent controversial, avant-garde production in New York announced to the audience that the intermission of the play would start when the actors and audience cleared the stage, someone was heard to shout from the audience: "What actors? What stage? What play?"

A first step in writing about a work of literature is to begin with the work on its own terms. Asked what poetry was, Robert Frost once responded, "Poetry is the kind of thing poets write." The definition may have been facetiously given but it wisely takes into account that our understanding of what a poem is, or of any other genre for that matter, must be able to change. Nevertheless, even though we should attempt to be receptive to changing forms, we do accumulate certain expectations as a result of our reading. Anyone who has read Dickens, Conrad, and Dostoevsky forms notions of what a novel is. These notions actually become the basis for making other judgments. If anyone thinks Keats's "Ode on a Grecian Urn" is close to a perfect poem, then the qualities of that poem shape his thinking about other ones. The touchstone method is practically unavoidable as a method of criticism. But it should also alert us to the fact that touchstones change and need to change. Students today are more likely to hold to Hesse or Nabokov as touchstones for the novel than to Conrad or Hardy. These changes are in part changes in taste and fashion, but we should not immediately assume that the present always supplants the past. Sophocles and Shakespeare, though they wrote centuries ago, remain perennially popular; furthermore, it is not the schools that are solely responsible for their endurance, even though these writers do, of course, regularly find a place in the curriculum. Poets of their stature survive simply because their forms and substance are incomparably durable.

In the present age that seems eagerly devoted to all kinds of change, it has been observed that people may not so much be seeking new forms as they are seeking new substance in old forms. Others may hold that no wise artist puts new wine in old bottles. Others may say that no old form can persist unchanged. Even if a poet writes a modern epic, he is not likely to follow the tradition of Vergil Dante, Spenser, and Milton. He will emulate the spirit of the epic tradition in the modes of his own time. Epics are still being written, but essentially in novel form. The novel is the contemporary counterpart of the poetic epic. What a development of this kind may suggest is that completely new forms are not so likely to emerge as that old forms shift, divide, and fuse so that more flexible categories emerge. Knowledge of the past, therefore, will continue to serve both the creative artist and the writer who is seeking to understand what the artist is doing. The writer about literature will do best first to know what the components of literature are and then see how they are treated by a particular writer in a work that has a purpose of its own. We will therefore discuss, in turn, character, action, setting, form, language, style, and meaning as the seven major components of literature, seeing how each functions in fiction, drama, and poetry and seeing how traditional concepts about literature may be undergoing reevaluation.

2

Character

Literary characters are those creations that permit artists to play deity—to populate a fictional universe with people and creatures of their own making. This power of creativity exceeds man's capacity to reproduce, for in physical reproduction the offspring is determined by natural law and heredity. The imagination can exceed those bounds; it can permit man to create what his body cannot. Early mythology is filled with hybrid beings—part woman and part serpent, part man and part goat, part woman, lion, and bird. Of course the imaginative power of a writer is not measured by his capacity to create the grotesque, but by his ability to shape with words an artistic world so that readers will view it with credibility.

If the world of a story is pure fantasy, the author must describe it so that readers believe imaginatively what they have not seen. If there are people who are unfamiliar, he must reveal them or let them reveal themselves by their words and actions so that readers know them. Unless characters say something, do something, interact, or have something happen to them, they are no more than mannequins on display. Within the confines of a novel's length or a play's duration, the writer causes us to identify and involve ourselves emotionally with his characters or to withdraw ourselves from them and look at them with detachment and criticism or to react to them indifferently. An indifferent response

17

by the reader is a sign either that the artist has failed or that the reader has failed to take into consideration what the writer has intended to do. At times, it is difficult to decide in modern works whether the writer is inviting us to believe in his characters or to laugh at their absurdities. Perhaps in a paradoxical way one can do both.

The Independent Life of Characters

One of the major misjudgments which many readers make about literature is to measure all characters by a single standard: their lifelikeness. Characters are not all alike and cannot be written about as if they were living creatures who exist in our own private surroundings. It matters little whether Macbeth would be a good or bad next-door neighbor; it does matter that he betrayed King Duncan for his own self-interest. It matters little whether the mad Ophelia would be good fun at a local party; it does matter that the fragile girl has understandably collapsed under the burdens which confront her in the play. In short, literary characters must be considered in their own literary environments, and the reader must consider the nature of the story before he dismisses any character as "unreal," "unbelievable," or "unlikely" because "people don't act that way." In writing about literature, we need to take into account different kinds of characters, the dimensions they assume, and the roles they are given in any particular story or play.

Stereotypes

A stereotype is a conventional character representing a particular group or class or occupation. Because the character is conventional, he acts according to set patterns. His appearance is familiar; his speech predictable; his actions standardized. Thus anyone who has read a story or seen an old movie knows how to impersonate a southern gentleman, a Jewish mamma, or a British lord with the aid of only a few gestures, props, and speech intonations. Imitations of this kind border on caricature; that is, they take identifiable characteristics of people and exaggerate them. People get classified by this means.

All stereotyping, of course, is not caricature; it can be a simplified way of looking at people as representatives of a group rather than as individuals. In Giraudoux's *The Madwoman of Chaillot* the cast includes characters such as The President, The Ragpicker, The

Prospector, The Doorman, and The Sewer Man, all unnamed, identified only by their rank or occupation. Yet these are not wholly wooden characters. Stereotypes often seem true to experience, not because they are exact replicas of people who walk the streets but because people whom we meet show some of the same traits of talking, dressing, and acting associated with types: hard sell with salesmen, flashy clothes with dudes, and shuffling with cowboys. Unquestionably, stereotypes in literature and other art forms have had their effect on social attitudes, often with serious and unjust consequences. Stereotyping conditions the way we look at one another, so that we tend to see a type that may not be at all accurate. Such typing is, obviously, a superficial way of looking at people.

Despite the serious social and personal implications of stereotyping, it persists in literature as a quick means of characterization. The typical senator, the typical Texan, the typical evangelist —these are all characterizations that may be used by a writer for a purpose, perhaps for comedy or satire. Because background characters of a story or drama make only brief appearances, they may have to be made recognizable quickly by typing devices. Bertolt Brecht, the German playwright and producer, knowing that typing sets the audience's expectations and dulls human perception, often defied physical stereotypes by deliberately avoiding type casting: calling for cooks who were thin, statesmen who were undignified, and lovers who were ugly. He wished to have the audience respond to the characters as presented, not in terms of preconceptions of them.

To label a literary figure as a type does not provide an individual much material for writing, but it does help as a starter if one can estimate how far beyond the typical a particular characterization moves. The Nurse in *Romeo and Juliet*, for example, could have been only a functional type, performing routine duties and making brief, innocuous responses. As it is, she does far more, but this limited conception of a servant role in other plays makes clear how far Shakespeare went to create an individual and colorful character who defies the conventions of her role.

Stock Characters

Closely related to stereotypes are stock characters. Even though the word "stock" has close associations with drama, stock figures appear in other genres as well. They are figures who because of their customary association with a dramatic situation have become conventions. Thus in Ovid's elegies, a young wife and a secret lover are haunted by the jealous eyes of an old and repulsive husband. These are stock figures who have been recast with variations over and over again throughout literature. The triangle situation is, of course, perennial. The philandering husband is as common as the erring young wife within the triangle.

Today we tend to identify the stock villain with the snarling, moustachioed character of nineteenth-century melodrama, but that figure is only an exaggerated portrayal of a long tradition of dark villains, including giants, misers, and magicians who pervade even the early mythology and literature. Among other stock characters, one could talk of traditional fools, scapegoats, sworn brothers, and fallen women. These traditions, which can be traced wherever and whenever a written literature is still extant, are a fascinating study, but they are not indispensable for understanding characters in any particular story or play. To see how Falstaff is a variation of a stock comic figure of the braggart soldier in Roman comedy or how Hamlet fits into the tradition of the revenge hero helps the reader to come to a deeper understanding of Shakespeare's powers of characterization, but this knowledge is not necessary to respond to these characters as they are revealed in the play.

Stock figures need not be typically portrayed. Willy Loman in Arthur Miller's *Death of a Salesman* might be considered the stock figure of the traveling salesman, but Miller does not treat Willy Loman in stock situations. Even though the world of salesmanship has been his whole life, the play itself focuses on Willy's private life as a husband and father. As a consequence, *Death of a Salesman* seldom permits the audience to cater to its stock responses. Willy Loman is one of the most pathetic of modern characters—a far departure from the prototype of the salesman in the common joke.

Allegorical and Symbolical Characters

In a letter to Sir Walter Ralegh, the English poet Edmund Spenser explained that he intended the long poem he was going to write to be read as an allegory. It would tell stories about knights who would represent the moral virtues set down by Aristotle, and Arthur himself would represent Magnificence, the perfection of all the other virtues. The poem he was planning became *The Faerie Queene*, written over a period of many years and never completed. The poem was not done exactly as Spenser described it to Ralegh, but his basic intention of writing an allegory did not change. Thus the incidents of the poem tell a story not only of knightly adventures but also of moral and political struggles. Many of the characters in the poem have obvious counterparts in the political world of the 1500s, and they can be aligned on the side of good or evil, as Spenser sees them. His allegory was a protective cloak in an age when criticism could seldom be spoken forthrightly. John Bunyan, a prose writer of the seventeenth century, also allegorizes throughout his long work *The Pilgrim's Progress*. It is the story of a Christian man's search for salvation. Its central character is called Christian by name, and his travels lead him finally to the Celestial City. On his journey, he encounters figures like Giant Despair, Mrs. Diffidence, Neighbor Pliable, and Neighbor Obstinate, all of whom personify the obstacles to virtuous living.

In works as obviously allegorical as Spenser's and Bunyan's, the reader's response to the characters is shaped by the nature of the work. But it does not follow that all allegorical figures are two-dimensional, cardboard personifications. In depicting the temptations of life, for instance, Bunyan is often as incisive in his brief characterizations as early painters like Brueghel were successful in depicting the sins of mankind on vast canvases populated by hundreds of allegorical figures. The characters of allegory can be as cartoonlike as Orwell's menagerie in *Animal Farm* or as lively and intense as the children in Golding's *Lord of the Flies* or as dramatic and memorable as the seamen of Melville's *Moby Dick*.

The author's allegorical intentions may at times help to explain the motivations and actions of his characters. Any character may be interpreted as symbolical when it appears that his actions and words seem designed to represent some thought or view or quality. A character is not symbolical unless he is symbolical *of* something. Thus the strange and unearthly Mélisande in Maeterlinck's play *Pelléas and Mélisande* seems to symbolize a pure innocence, a fragile quality like Mélisande herself, who cannot survive in the world she inhabits.

Yet all characters who are representative are not symbolical. Even though Holden Caulfield in *The Catcher in the Rye* may epitomize the attitudes of his age group, one cannot think of him in any way as symbolical. Ultimately, a symbolical figure is one whose accumulated actions lead the reader to see him as something more than his own person, to see him perhaps as the embodiment of pure barbarism or redemptive power or hope. In these terms, the symbolical nature of a character may at times grow beyond the author's original intentions, but an author, once he has created his characters, no longer controls them. The reader is free to see symbolical implications in a character if the evidence within the literary work itself supports such a reading. Symbolical interpretation is forced when the reader deliberately distorts to arrive at what he considers profound implications. A reader ordinarily does not need to ferret out symbolical characters. Their illusiveness and mystery usually announce them and invite explanation.

Full-Dimensional Characters

Just as individuals interest us more than masses of people representing movements, so also the full-dimensional characters of literature have attracted most of the attention to themselves. They are described at greater length and revealed in more detail; they are capable of greater individuation. No doubt, many people whom we encounter casually and see only as stereotypes—the waitress, the cab driver, the elevator operator—would be interesting subjects for study, but, just as in life, literature does not permit us to know every character equally well. Leading characters of a literary work are drawn in full; other figures are sketched in to fill out the scene. Although poetry ordinarily does not permit the same space for character development that fiction and drama do, it still manages by implication to suggest the full dimensionality of its characters. T. S. Eliot creates the memorable figure of Prufrock in only 131 lines; Chaucer uses only 32 for the Wife of Bath.

Nevertheless, the very length of fiction and drama permits the possibility of presenting characters who grow and change over a period of time. A novelist like Dickens very often accounted for the full lifespan of his characters, from birth to death, even though his story might focus mainly on one period. The final chapter of *Oliver Twist* gives an accounting of "the fortunes of those who have figured in this tale. . . ." A long novel following a character through many years, through many experiences at different ages, allows us to know him as intimately as we know only those who are closest to us. And the probing of a twentieth-century author like James Joyce into the inner minds and motivations of characters permits us to know them even more intimately than we know our friends. Literature gives us an opportunity to stop the life of a character, to turn back pages, to reread, to reflect, to examine motivations, to be involved and detached at one and the same time; and, after the story has been completed, to reconsider those thoughts and feelings we have accumulated in the course of the novel. Seldom do we think of any living person's actions in such detail, even our own. Literature is a public view of private matters; it is both open and intimate.

Yet space, detail, and full-dimensionality alone do not create a Madame Bovary, a Raskolnikov, or a Studs Lonigan. The great characters of literature are those who constantly recreate themselves in the imaginations of readers. They are not limited to durable types of perennially symbolic figures. They are individuals who can be seen coping with other men or destiny or God or themselves. They may fail, but they embody human strengths and weaknesses and man's undying impulse to be himself, even if it is not the highest self of which he is capable. Readers do not permit characters who embody man's essential nature to fade away, because the expression of true human individuality in literature and life is all too rare.

The Permanence and Universality of Characters

The permanence of literary characters in their written form raises a question about their true nature. They are persistent and stable because they cannot change; only readers can change their attitudes about them. They continue to live on for centuries, whereas men die. Yet we constantly distinguish fictional characters from real men, implying that their reality is of a different nature. Indeed it is, but not necessarily of an inferior nature. Literary characters are limited by the qualities and situations and scenes given to them by the author to live over and over again, but they enjoy an earthly immortality which men achieve only by also becoming, like them, characters in history books, novels, and biographies.

Nevertheless, the permanence of fictional characters is tenuous. It is dependent on more than the durability of the manuscript on which the character is recorded. Granted that manuscripts and their contents can always be reproduced (what likelihood is there that *Huckleberry Finn* will be lost to subsequent generations?), volumes of books continue to exist either as inert museum pieces or as vital creations. Literary figures must constantly experience an imaginative revival in the minds of men to gain their immortality. In this respect they are subject to the whims of men. Only those characters who continue to meet the test of future generations become the truly universal figures.

Characters are not universal in the sense that they are everybody. A character who is everyman is probably no man at all, only a symbol. A universal character is first a person whose qualities can be generalized. Not many men, like Oedipus, kill their fathers and marry their mothers. His particular circumstances are not the bond between him and us, but his reactions are. Given equally catastrophic circumstances, how does any man respond? Does he feel within himself Oedipus' stubborn resistance to fate and show his persistence to dig out the truth? Oedipus is a man of pride and guilt and grief who comes to realize the consequences of his acts and his role as a man of fate. These are dilemmas which many men have not solved for themselves. The tragedy of Oedipus teaches them and involves them in an experience that warns them to fear for themselves.

Paradoxically, a writer cannot guarantee the universality of his creations. He can only attempt to create an individual who he hopes will continue to appeal to subsequent generations. Once separated from the author's mind in the form that he gives it, a literary character begins an independent existence. Like a Falstaff, he can assume an importance that the author probably never intended. Like a Shylock, a stereotype can undergo a complete metamorphosis. Therefore, any reader of a new day holds the capacity to see a literary figure in a new perspective. Anyone writing about literature needs to realize that the final word can never be said about the truly great figures of literature.

Functions of Characters

What also cannot change about literary characters is their relationships to each other within their own fictional universe. A new generation's attitude may change toward matters like adultery, rebellion, and pride, but it cannot alter how the author has structured his characters to reveal their qualities.

In almost any literary work, several characters receive the main focus. Accordingly, they are considered the leading characters or protagonists. When no character receives such an emphasis, as in Hauptmann's *The Weavers* or Gorky's *The Lower Depths,* it is customary to state that the people as a whole—as a force or movement—are the author's central interest.

But given a protagonist, the conflict of a story may depend on the existence of an antagonist. Hamlet's rivalry with King Claudius makes that drama a struggle for survival between "mighty equals." In other instances, like Stephen Crane's *The Open Boat,* the antagonist is a natural element—the unconquerable sea. With varying degrees of emphasis, the sea or the desert or the mountains or the elements can assume such a role.

A foil is a character who serves as a contrast to another, usually in such a way as to work to the advantage of the leading character. At times, the foil may also be the antagonist, as Hotspur is to Henry IV in Shakespeare's history play or even as Laertes, a foil to Hamlet, eventually becomes his antagonist. One of the most memorable of all foils is Sancho Panza, the earthy companion of the lofty-minded Don Quixote in Cervantes' novel.

Familiarity with even these few examples will suggest that,

though a foil may be intended to enhance the reader's opinion of the protagonist, the reader may actually prefer the foil. His nature may be more compatible with the reader's own temperament and views. This kind of reaction can be a subject for writing, particularly if the writer can explain how his own personal reaction to a particular character affects his attitude toward the total work that has probably been constructed to gain sympathy for the protagonist.

A confidant, often used in drama, is a character to whom the protagonist reveals his inner thoughts; he becomes a convenient device for the protagonist to speak his thoughts to without addressing them to the audience in the form of a soliloquy. Thus, Hamlet, who at times does soliloquize, takes Horatio into his confidence. If the confidant himself plays an active role in the play, then his own character serves as a commentary upon the protagonist in the same way that the foil represents a contrast. In many instances, however, the confidant is only a passive character, perhaps a servant or close friend, whose main purpose is to listen, not to advise or influence the main character.

A narrator is consistently a special kind of character because, in fiction, he either shapes the entire story by his point of view or, in drama, he acts as a kind of one-man chorus commenting on the action. The narrator may play a double role; that is, he may actually be a character in a particular set of circumstances, and he may also be the one who at some future time chooses to tell the story in which he was involved. Thus, Melville's *Moby Dick* begins with the words, "Call me Ishmael." Ishmael is the narrator. He is also a seaman who accompanies Ahab in the pursuit of the white whale and survives. Ishmael is therefore a character in the novel who is as subject to analysis as any other character. On the other hand, the narrator in Thornton Wilder's *Our Town,* even though he is one of the townspeople, views the dramatic scene as if it were framed. He is identified as a stage manager and plays that role. At various times, he narrates the history of the characters; he interrupts the action to shift the scene; he communicates with the living and the dead; he philosophizes. He is a wise, interested observer, but one whose special role as stage manager and narrator and chorus makes him a unique character.

Finally, in almost all stories and plays there are background characters who populate the scene. Ordinarily these are of no special interest unless, as a mass, they assume an active role. In Ibsen's *An Enemy of the People,* the people as a group are the antagonists of Dr. Stockmann. He is the individual who has to stand up against the many. They are the composite economic society; they are the ones who want to maintain their investments even at the expense of human life. As individuals, they are not greatly differentiated. But as people in a community they can be discussed as if they were one.

Methods of Characterization

Because of the fixed nature of literary characters, writing about them depends to a great extent on being able to seek out meaningful clues and determine what techniques the writer has used to reveal his characters. In character analysis, it is helpful to begin with the assumption that a character is coherently developed. This assumption does not necessarily mean that the complete characterization exists in the author's mind before he ever begins, for we have the testimony of authors that characters grow in their minds as they write and even, at times, escape their control, seemingly creating their own lives. Characters may change within the course of a story or play and still be coherent. But the idea of a coherent character does assume that certain values and motives and beliefs—a kind of functional philosophy—cause a character to act and speak in a particular way; and, if he deviates, he is performing inconsistently or he has changed his value system. Interpretations about motivation and action will vary, of course. Much discussion about a complex character like Hamlet hinges to a great extent on differences of opinion about his madness or his feigned madness and the extent to which he fully controls his words and actions, to what extent he is deliberate and purposeful, to what extent he is frenzied and impulsive.

Even though we can assume that artistic creations are coherent, a careful reader will nevertheless approach characterization inductively, beginning first with details of characterization and then coming to some conclusions about the elements of coherence: Are a character's actions adequately explained? Are they justified by the causes for them? Do his responses seem consistent with the things we learn about him? Literature provides a map of character. We can trace the starting points, the directions, and the destination. The whole terrain is laid out to be viewed and examined. Intuitions about fictional characters can be trustworthy or completely misleading; character analysis itself depends on a presentation of detailed evidence about a character with the intention of seeing him as a whole being.

The Actions of Characters

Clearly, the reader has to be alert to the actions of a character because actions are the author's way of showing, not telling, what his characters are like. Yet surface appearances must be questioned. In one scene of Melville's *Benito Cereno,* Babo appears to be a faithful servant shaving Don Benito in the presence of Captain Delano, the visiting captain aboard ship. At that moment, however, Babo, with razor in hand, is actually terrorizing Don Benito in order to keep him silent. The suspense of a story like Melville's *Benito Cereno* depends on the unsuspecting nature of the American Captain Delano, who is deceived by what he sees and through whom we as readers view the scene. Only when at the end of the story Babo jumps into a boat in an effort to kill the escaping captain is Delano's deception illuminated. In an instant, his mind moves to review all of the previous events in the light of a newly discovered truth that the slaves have mutinied and already massacred most of the Spanish crew.

Written during a period when the antislavery movement in America was strong and the reactions to slave revolts were sometimes sympathetic and sometimes hostile, Melville's story raises the question whether he is taking a stand on the slavery issue. Is Babo a heroic rebel or a monstrous murderer? An abolitionist would favor the first interpretation. But one answer given in terms of the literal narrative about a slave mutiny changes if Melville intended the story to be read as a moral allegory, as many of his stories are. Then the characters need to be interpreted in terms of symbols, especially the color symbols. In the story, black seems clearly symbolic of evil and white of good; in these terms, Babo becomes a depraved leader. Obviously, Black readers today would find this symbolism and this interpretation distasteful, but apart from the historical context the work can stand on its own. Critics are not in complete agreement about Melville's intentions, but what is apparent is that the reader can see Babo as either good or evil; one interpretation or the other simply emphasizes different kinds of evidence.

The Appearance of Characters

In some stories and plays, the appearance of a character may be taken as a clue to his nature if the author leads the reader to attach significance to it. Most people today tend to look on ugliness and distortion without suspicion, but in times past outer flaws were taken as a sign of inner corruption. From early childhood, fairy tales and mythological stories have conditioned us to accept the literary fact that dwarfs and witches and monstrous creatures are servants of evil, and heroes and heroines are handsome, beautiful, and good. The world of the fairy tale is one of simple contrasts.

Yet, even when the fictional universe is not quite so simplified and stories are not told to enforce moral platitudes, writers continue to attach significance to physical appearance. The brief sketches in the Prologue to Chaucer's *Canterbury Tales* consistently include descriptions of physical details and dress which give significant indexes to character and social station. Chaucer's description of the Squire includes the line, "Short was his gowne, with sleves longe and wyde"—usually understood to be details that indicate the Squire was dressed in the very latest fashion. Chaucer describes him as a young and lusty fellow, gaily dressed, and full of spirit—a sharp contrast to the divinity student, the Clerk, whose coat is threadbare and whose horse is as lean as a rake.

Shakespeare uses appearance in a play like *Richard III* as a psychological motivation. In the opening soliloquy of the play, Richard reveals the thoughts about his deformity that prey upon his mind, finally declaring:

And therefore, since I cannot prove a lover,
To entertain these fair well-spoken days,
I am determined to prove a villain
And hate the idle pleasures of these days.

Thus, from the outset Richard's physical ugliness is announced as a motive for his monstrous actions.

In *Hedda Gabler*, Ibsen provides clues to the interpretation of characters in the brief description he includes in the stage directions at their first entrance. When Hedda enters, Ibsen assumes the part of a narrator: "Her steel-gray eyes express a cold, unruffled response. Her hair is of an agreeable medium brown, but not particularly abundant." When Mrs. Tesman, Hedda's foil and rival, enters, Ibsen writes, "Her eyes are light blue, large, round, and somewhat prominent, with a startled, inquiring expression. Her hair is remarkably light, almost flaxen, and unusually abundant and wavy." If one ignores these contrasting characteristics, he ignores how Ibsen defines the relationship between the two women from the very beginning and how, in particular, the references to hair and stroking hair and pulling hair at scattered points throughout the play are intended as significant clues to Hedda's character.

The Speech of Characters

It is axiomatic that what characters speak ought to be important in learning about them. There is a tendency, however, in reading (as opposed to listening) to concentrate on the what and the why —the substance and purpose—and to pay less attention to the when and the how—the occasion and the manner. In writing about a character's speeches, an interpreter has to attempt to project himself into the character: How would he say the words? What are his habits of speech? What is his tone? Does the occasion color the tone? Answering these questions can provide possible insights into meaning, especially extrasensory meaning, which always represents another level of nonverbal communication. When people are speaking, they are also gesturing, grimacing, inflecting the voice, stressing, and in numerous subtle ways influencing the meaning, adding to it, and, when they are being ironic, even reversing the meaning. All of these extrasensory implications have to be inferred from the reading. A fictional narrator may add a few introductory details to a speech, telling how it was spoken, but the reader is still left to interpret. In drama, the whole matter is taken over by actor and director. It is therefore not at all unusual that different readings of identical roles by different individuals can produce a totally different conception of a character. The rhythms can be slowed or quickened. The lines can be consistently twisted for humor or satire. All of the speeches can be heightened or understated. Nevertheless, the original author by his choice of words, usages, structures, and rhetorical devices builds into the speeches a core of meaning and effect which in itself cannot be altered but can be developed as the interpreter sees fit, consistent with his total interpretation of the character.

Two strikingly different examples out of context will illustrate what kinds of elements are built into speeches. The first is a speech from a play; the second is a line of dialogue from a novel:

CHARACTER 1

Mount, mount, my soul! Thy seat is up on high,
Whilst my gross flesh sinks downward, here to die.

CHARACTER 2

"Don't worry, darling. . . . I'm not a bit afraid. It's just a dirty trick."

What is first obvious is that there is a different rhetoric operating in each speech. It is unlikely that Character 1, even in his own person, could speak Character 2's line. Not only is the meaning a part of the style—the characteristic thoughts of the character—but the manner also. The first speech seems to be a dramatic, oratorical apostrophe of the character to his soul at the moment of death. The second is calm and intimate, addressed to another person—a completely different approach to death, since these are also words spoken at the moment before dying. Having to die is the "dirty trick."

Thus, knowing the occasion throws considerable light on the implications of the second speech, but the intimate elements are built in. It cannot be delivered in the manner of the first, because the structures and words do not lend themselves to that treatment. Yet each speech, within the limits of its language, can be interpreted to show different qualities about the characters at the moment of their death. Character 1 could be seen as noble and high-minded or as pompous and shallow. Character 2 could be seen as casual and superficial or as brave and bitter. Or perhaps these are not the exact descriptive adjectives at all in terms of the total characterization and the occasion; they explain only possible effects. Yet we do know that the speeches identify two characters of quite different temperament, and the speeches contain clues to the characterization.

Character 1 is actually King Richard II in Shakespeare's play of that name. Richard has been forced to abdicate and has been replaced on the throne by Bolingbroke (Henry IV). He is imprisoned in Pomfret Castle, reflecting at length upon the discontent of his life, daily fearing that his food will be poisoned to end his life. Death, ironically, comes as a rude assault. Men break in, slay the guards, and strike Richard down. In his dying words, Richard damns his slayer and, in a final gesture of kingliness, cries out

> Mount, mount, my soul! Thy seat is up on high,
> Whilst my gross flesh sinks downward here to die.

His slayer is moved to speak:

> As full of valor as of royal blood.

Character 2 is Catherine Barkley in Hemingway's *A Farewell to Arms*. She is an English nurse serving in World War I. Her lover is Frederic Henry, an American lieutenant attached to an Italian ambulance unit. In the final scene of the novel, Frederic takes Catherine to a hospital where she gives birth to his child. The baby is dead; she knows she is dying and says she hates it. She tries to reassure Frederic, kidding him a bit, vacillating between thoughts of loving and dying. When a doctor directs Frederic to go out of the room, the novel records the scene with simplicity:

> "Don't worry, darling," Catherine said. "I'm not a bit afraid. It's just a dirty trick."

They are her last words. They too are "full of valor as of royal blood," but her bravery and nobility are of a different variety.

These two brief speeches do reveal character. Because they are dying speeches, they are particularly important ones. But what each reveals, it reveals less by what it says literally than by the way the words are spoken, to whom they are addressed, when, and under what circumstances.

Almost identical words can be interpreted differently when they are considered in a total context. For example, the terrified Johnny in Sean O'Casey's *Juno and the Paycock,* about to be dragged out and killed, reverts to ritual:

> Sacred Heart of Jesus, have mercy on me! Mother o'God, pray for me— be with me now in the agonies o' death! . . . Hail, Mary, full o' grace . . . The Lord is . . . with Thee.

In Eliot's *Murder in the Cathedral,* Thomas Becket, Archbishop of England, about to be slain, speaks to those around him:

> Now to the Almighty God, to the Blessed Mary, ever Virgin, to the blessed John the Baptist, the holy apostles Peter and Paul, to the blessed martyr Denys, and to all the Saints, I commend my cause and that of the Church.

One ritualistic speech reveals misery and desperation; the other courage and affirmation; yet these are impressions that are derived from more than the meanings of the words themselves. Characters in stories and plays seldom make formal addresses about themselves; their speeches are indexes, but their lives need to be interpreted dramatically, for to ignore the total context may be to distort the interpretation.

The Persona of the Poet

Poems, like plays and stories, are sometimes written about people, and we feel essentially the same interest in these characters as we do in other ones in fiction and drama, except that we are seldom provided with the same kind of detail which permits us to understand them as fully developed characters. These, however, are the visible and identifiable characters of a poem. But like the narrator of a story or the director of a play who remains behind the scenes, a similar kind of character frequently appears in a poem. He is the character whose voice we hear but do not see in person. He is the author in the role he chooses to assume rather than speak in his own voice. This voice is ordinarily referred to as the persona of the poet or the persona of the poem.

In Edwin Arlington Robinson's poem "Luke Havergal," the speaker, the "I" of the poem, is clearly not the author:

> Go to the western gate, Luke Havergal,
> There where the vines cling crimson on the wall,
> And in the twilight wait for what will come.
> The leaves will whisper there for her, and some,
> Like flying words, will strike you as they fall;
> But go, and if you listen she will call.
> Go to the western gate, Luke Havergal—
> Luke Havergal.

No, there is not a dawn in eastern skies
To rift the fiery night that's in your eyes;
But there, where western glooms are gathering,
The dark will end the dark, if anything:
God slays Himself with every leaf that flies,
And hell is more than half of paradise.
No, there is not a dawn in eastern skies—
In eastern skies.

Out of a grave I come to tell you this,
Out of a grave I come to quench the kiss
That flames upon your forehead with a glow
That blinds you to the way that you must go.
Yes, there is yet one way to where she is,
Bitter, but one that faith may never miss.
Out of a grave I come to tell you this—
To tell you this.

There is the western gate, Luke Havergal,
There are the crimson leaves upon the wall.
Go, for the winds are tearing them away,—
Nor think to riddle the dead words they say,
Nor any more to feel them as they fall;
But go, and if you trust her she will call.
There is the western gate, Luke Havergal—
Luke Havergal.

The outlines of the dramatic situation seem fairly clear: a girl whom Luke has loved has died; he is left in bewilderment, not knowing what to do. It is then that a voice both commands and lures him to "go to the western gate." Who is the figure who comes "out of a grave" to tell him this? Is it Death himself? Or Death's agent? Or is it merely an inner voice within Luke that tells him to follow her by killing himself? There are no definite answers as to who the voice is, but any interpretation of the poem must attempt to account for it in some way.

The importance of the persona will, of course, vary from poem to poem, but, after a first reading, one should always attempt to resolve in his own mind who the speaker is. If it is not the author, then the persona is functioning as a dramatic character, assuming a role that is integral to an understanding of the dramatic conflict and meaning of the poem.

SUGGESTIONS FOR WRITING ABOUT CHARACTERS

Characters are the focus of almost any literary work of a dramatic nature. No one needs to direct attention to them as subjects for writing, but it is not always equally as clear what one writes *about* in analyzing characters. Literary analysis is not pure description or a summary of the action, although it may include elements of these. It is not gossip—the nature of much of our talk about living people. It is more in the nature of amateur psychoanalysis which concerns itself with the way a character acts and talks, with the reasons he acts as he does, or with the way parts of his life fit together to create a total impression. The writer's job, above all, is to convey to the reader his understanding of the character and the character's role in a literary work. He may want to approach the analysis diagnostically, looking at the symptoms and signs which lead to a particular conclusion. A character analysis of this sort may set out to prove a kind of thesis, such as: Nora in Ibsen's *A Doll's House* is a nineteenth-century forerunner of the twentieth-century feminist and career woman, or Henry Fleming in *The Red Badge of Courage* is a central figure in a story about Christian redemption. The first thesis would look at Nora from the perspective of a different age, but it would still be an analysis limited to what actually happens in the play. The second thesis would emphasize how the novel works out a general theme through its characters—Henry's relation to Jim Conklin, for instance. Topics of this variety indicate that it is rarely possible to write about characters without referring to many other elements that go to make up the literary work.

Another approach to writing about character comes close to a completely personal view, because essentially it is a reader's attempt to get at the nature of a character by an impressionistic sketch. This kind of character analysis is clearly more speculative and intuitive than the first, but it can at times be successful in describing the emotional temperament of a character.

However varied written papers about characters may be, they ought to be true to the details that the author gives about a character in the special fictional world that has been created. Questions like the following will help the reader come to some understanding of literary characterization as opposed to his usual casual assessment of people in daily life:

1. Into what categories do the characters of a story or drama fall? Are they types? Are some clearly individualized and fully developed?
2. In what ways do characters comment on one another either by their words or their actions? Are they grouped so that they form contrasting views or attitudes or values?
3. What is the author trying to do with particular characters? What is his chief intention? To reveal the variety of human nature? To use characters as mouthpieces for his own ideas? To show a certain style of living? To illustrate a theme through them?
4. Is the characterization of the protagonist coherent? Are his actions motivated? Are some actions unexplainable in terms of the character or of the continuing story?
5. Does the time span of the action allow for a developing character? What changes take place in the thinking of a character? Why?
6. How do we learn to know the characters? How well? What typical techniques does the author use to reveal character? In what special ways do actions and appearances add to our knowledge of a character?

7. What details about a character seem to give him or her universal appeal? What particular elements are dated?
8. Do you look sympathetically or critically on the characters? What in the literary characterization and action affects you to respond one way or the other? Do you identify or sympathize with a character who in the construction of the plot seems not to invite sympathy?
9. In what way do minor characters fit into the total scheme of the story? Why couldn't they be omitted?
10. How do the characters speak?

3

Action

Things that happen—actions—continue to be a major factor in literature. We might echo one of the great literary passages of Ecclesiastes in the Bible to say that in literature there is a season for everything: "A time to be born and a time to die . . . a time to kill and a time to heal . . . a time to weep and a time to laugh, a time to mourn and a time to lament . . . a time to get and a time to lose . . . a time to love and a time to hate, a time of war and a time of peace."

When Aristotle discussed tragedy in the *Poetics*, one of the earliest and most influential critical works written, he placed prime importance on plot. To him, plot was not the story or the actions alone; it was also the arrangement of the incidents. The same story might be told by a number of different plots.

If we reflect on Aristotle's preference and then think of contemporary writing in terms of the seven elements of literature we are discussing—character, action, setting, form, language, style, and meaning—we would distort considerably if we said that writers today seem primarily concerned with plot and action. Some writers like George Bernard Shaw and Katherine Anne Porter seem little concerned with plot. In contrast to earlier stories, plays, and poems, a remarkably static quality seems to pervade much of current literature. Characters no longer do things; rather, they talk, not always to others but often to themselves, or they reflect upon the things they have done or they contemplate the actions they might have taken but did not. If the description seems also to fit a character like Hamlet, we need to remind ourselves that Shakespeare in that play was basically writing his version of a revenge drama. At the end, the stage is strewn with dead bodies.

Action is no longer even the heart of narrative. The clear exception, of course, is the murder mysteries, spy stories, science fiction tales, westerns, gothic tales, and historical novels that are constantly produced in huge numbers; these still feature adventures, searches, accidents, and chases. Aside from these works, however, a modern Aristotle observing today's tragedies and other forms would be hard pressed to consider plot of primary importance.

The Events

As simple as it is to ask the question, What is happening? it is by no means easy to answer it. The reader's first obligation is to be as clear as he can about the sequence of events. In long narrative poems and novels and plays, the events may be fairly well defined and expanded. The more compressed the form or the more oblique the point of view, however, the more difficult it is to establish the narrative sequence. Readers accustomed to rapid narration will no doubt encounter considerable trouble with Faulkner's "Barn Burning," merely trying to establish what is happening. Or in Pirandello's *Six Characters in Search of an Author,* in which the events are fragmented as if the author tossed the pieces of a puzzle in the air to leave them where they fell, one clue to understanding the drama fully is to arrange the events in the order in which they happened, not the order in which they are revealed. In Marvell's "To His Coy Mistress," some readers miss completely what is happening, because the poem itself is a lover's speech, but it is a speech being made to move his coy mistress to act with him like "amorous birds of prey." To miss the seduction that is going on is to miss a good bit of the irony.

Nevertheless, merely to summarize what is happening in any work is not advisable unless one suspects that he has discovered something that no one else has perceived. Determining the events is usually the spadework that one assumes of every writer before he begins. Yet student themes too often reveal that the writer has failed to start at this most basic level. If he has mastered the sequence of events, he can legitimately write about the kinds of changes in actions that take place. These observations are usually closely related to character analysis because in works of adequate length characters often grow and change, not always in terms of time, but in terms of realization and understanding. One can think of the relationship between actions and thoughts in two ways. First, actions sometimes influence characters. These are essentially forces beyond their control, like work, taxes, health, interpersonal relations, whatever affects them externally. On the other hand, a character himself often determines the action. Motivated by his own needs, desires, or ambitions, he shapes the things that occur. He causes actions; he is not acted upon. Inasmuch as the things that happen in a work of literature are the writer's invention, even though they may be based on actual fact, we are obliged to draw significance from actions, either as they happen to characters or as they are made to happen. They are clues to change and indications of the forces that are operating to cause them. What is happening or perhaps not happening is therefore one of the sources of learning what a story or play or poem is about.

The Selection of Events

The length of a work to a great extent determines what is included or omitted. Short stories ordinarily embrace a short span of time and limited situations. Poems may focus on the detail of a single event, sometimes on something of seemingly little importance, like the widening concentric circles caused by a pebble tossed into a pond. If a writer wants to write a short story, his choice of form may influence the scope of the action, or he may have the action in mind and choose a form appropriate to it. The epic and the novel (consider Milton's *Paradise Lost* and Tolstoy's *War and Peace*) hold the greatest potential for the panoramic. The drama is less compatible to the densely populated and shifting scene. Ibsen's *Peer Gynt,* for example, suffers from diffuseness. Goethe's *Faust* is essentially a reading drama, not easily adaptable to the theater. Shakespeare's *Antony and Cleopatra* is without doubt more successful in its revelation of the intimate love scenes between Antony and Cleopatra than it is in its depiction of the political and military events involving Antony, Octavius, and Lepidus.

During two main periods in literary history—the fifth century B.C. in Athens and the Renaissance on the Continent and in England—most dramatists restricted their plays to an observance of what are familiarly called the unities of place, time, and action, that is, limiting the action to one setting, covering a twenty-four-hour span, and using a single plot line, omitting contrasting or supporting subplots and other episodes not immediately necessary to the exposition of the drama proper. What dramas of this kind lost in their illusion of reality they often gained in the intensity of their effects through compression. In a similar way, short stories and poems that represent only a modicum of action may comment more deeply and meaningfully upon experience than novels and dramas of far broader scope.

Given the customary limits of the various forms, the writer is still left to include and omit what he wishes. The reader is left to infer that what the writer includes he includes for a purpose and what he omits he also omits by choice. Analysis of literature, therefore, involves the weighing of all details in relation to the total purpose. Why does Shakespeare have King Lear at the moment of the old man's supreme grief and tragedy concern himself with asking Albany to undo a button? Why does Browning have the Duke in "My Last Duchess" lead the envoy down the staircase and point out a particular statue done by Claus of Innsbruck? These are seemingly unimportant details of action, but the writers have included them at climactic points as touches of humanity or means of commentary. Such details of action cannot be ignored.

Focusing on Events

Both distortion and understatement are means of drawing attention to special events. Each is possible because each is a deviation in an opposite direction from what a reader customarily expects. From everyday experience, readers know in a very general way how things usually happen and how people react. This knowledge determines what we might call ordinary expectations. This is not to say that expectations about living and thinking do not change, but they clearly prevail among the majority of people at any particular time. A distortion of action or an understatement of effect, therefore, gets a special response from readers because they consider these changes improbable or unexpected.

Shakespeare's *Richard III* records the desperate measures of that monarch to secure his throne by conniving, imprisonment of enemies, and murder. But his efforts cannot offset the growing rebellion of the powerful lords of the realm. These are matters of historical record. But Shakespeare, although he was writing a play based on history, was not writing history. In scene iv of Act IV, he has a messenger arrive from Devonshire to report to Richard that Sir Edward Courtney and the Bishop of Exeter are in arms. Almost immediately, a second messenger arrives from Kent to report that the Guildfords are in arms. A third messenger enters to report the destruction of Buckingham's army; though this is a message favorable to Richard's cause, it is quickly offset by the arrival of a fourth messenger from Yorkshire who reports the disastrous news that Lovel and Dorset are also in rebellion. The distortion of the time element—the coincidence of these arrivals —becomes a dramatic means of conveying the impact of these events on Richard, and the compression of the time permits Shakespeare to have Richard stirred to immediate action against the rebels, saying,

> While we reason here
> A royal battle might be won and lost.

Here the depiction of the action is not historically accurate, but it is dramatically valid. A similar device of messengers arriving one after the other to report disasters is used also in the Biblical story of Job and retained by Archibald MacLeish in *J.B.*, his modern adaptation of the tale. In all three examples, the overwhelming effect of disaster becomes the test of a man.

Understatement of action also has its own shattering effect. We would be hard pressed to find a more skillful use than the ending of Katherine Anne Porter's *Pale Horse, Pale Rider*, a subtle story of young love during wartime. Miranda, snatched from death after a prolonged illness from influenza during the epidemic of 1918, turns finally to a collection of letters that she has willingly left unopened on her table. Encouraged to read them, she takes them in order—"What a victory, what triumph, what happiness to be alive, sang the letters in a chorus." But one of them is a thin letter notifying her that Adam her lover has died of influenza in a camp hospital. Miranda does not collapse. There is no emotional outburst, no hysteria, no cursing of fate. Porter's closing description of Miranda going about the business of telling a friend what few items she will again need—lipstick, gauntlets, stockings, and a walking stick—and then her awful sense of aloneness—these understated details of action are as overwhelming and dramatically moving as any piling up of effects. Katherine Anne Porter leaves the reader with a paralyzing sense of the irony of the story she has told:

> No more war, no more plague, only the dazed silence that follows the ceasing of the heavy guns; noiseless houses with the shades drawn, empty streets, the dead cold light of tomorrow. Now there would be time for everything.

Observations of this kind concerning action in a story or play reveal in what way a writer is influencing our thoughts and feelings. Since a literary work is not bound to fact or nature, a writer is free to alter people and circumstances to the extent that he dares. His skill in doing so may be his major claim to greatness.

A Complete Action

Like many other critical principles, the concept of what completeness is derives from Aristotle. Aristotle defined a whole as that which has a beginning, a middle, and an end; and he continued by specifying that a beginning is that which does not follow something else as a necessary result; an ending is that which naturally does follow other consequences; and a middle is something which naturally follows something else as something else in turn follows it. One may think that his definitions are too obvious even to be stated. Nevertheless, though his concept is a strong, inescapable part of our thinking about wholeness, its obviousness can no longer be taken for granted. For more than a hundred years at least, developments in art, music, and literature have been undermining the notion that a whole is that which has a beginning, a middle, and an end. We have come to recognize fragments as wholes, incompleteness as completeness, disorder as a kind of order, and endings as a convenience, not a necessity. The first of these new concepts is already firmly established in literature, and the others continue to make themselves evident in various writings that deviate sharply from conventional norms.

One of the clearest illustrations of the adjustment in our thinking about a fragment as a whole may be observed in our acceptance of what we now familiarly call slice-of-life dramas and stories. The phrase originated in the nineteenth century and now serves as a common descriptive term for plays and stories that do not attempt to account for beginnings and endings in the Aristotelian sense, that give us only a view of the middle—a passing scene through a window, an opening of a door upon a room, only to have it closed again without explanation; figuratively, a slice from the total lives of the characters involved. Thus, middles stand as wholes unless one insists that a whole must also have a beginning and an ending.

Obviously, every work of literature has some point of starting and stopping, and every work of literature in the same line of reasoning may be said to be only a segment of life. Yet these concepts of beginning and ending and the idea of slicing out a middle are quite different from the logical completeness that Aristotle speaks of. What we now read may be only a beginning or a middle or an ending, not necessarily all three. If a reader's aesthetic satisfaction depends upon having actions come to completion or complications fully resolved, if his aesthetic satisfaction depends upon perceiving the shape of a beginning and a middle and an end, then he will be constantly frustrated by much of the fragmented work that he encounters in modern literature, and in art and music as well.

The interrupted or unfinished or unpolished work is now praised, because in its incompleteness it is said to communicate less but suggest more. It has greater capacity to move us emotionally. The reader or viewer or listener must participate. It is possible that Dickens' unfinished novel *The Mystery of Edwin Drood* has prompted more imaginative speculation than all his other novels with their carefully worked out endings. If the mystery is to be solved, the reader must do it. One might consider the work finished, particularly since Dickens undoubtedly intended to finish it, but one can also entertain the idea that any writer might deliberately stop his work short of resolution, just as Puccini ended *Madama Butterfly* on an unresolved chord. That particular ending, even though it is not logically or aesthetically satisfying, comments on the action that comes before it, and its failure to satisfy does not make it less complete. One might argue that a work is complete if the author says it is.

In a similar vein, the fragmented and disorderly are now highly regarded as characteristic of man, nature, and society. Not even science as it continues to make new discoveries can cling to its former theories of an orderly universe. The question arises whether order actually does exist or whether it exists only in art or whether it represents a condition that man imposes upon the disorderliness of the world in which he lives. Perhaps disorder is the "natural order" of things—a paradox that only art can reflect. A novel by William Burroughs is no longer an easy progression from beginning to middle to end; it is a labyrinth that the reader must work his way through and out of, at the risk of being lost altogether.

Once the traditional concept of beginning, middle, and end is given up, then the well-made stories and plays, with their set incidents and coincidences and intrigues and solutions, become passé. Once the concept of beginning, middle, and end is relinquished, then the entire Western sense of time is somehow irrelevant to art. Things can continue indefinitely. The music of Messiaen and Cage is not conceived and shaped in terms of traditional time. In fact, Cage writes that music is not a set experience with a frame around it; it is constantly manifest in all of the sounds about us, including noise. It can be experienced by tuning in; formal pieces of music tend to lose the dynamic quality of life. Popular ballads no longer end; they fade out as if they continued on and on. Once the concept of beginning, middle, and end is disregarded, then the whole idea of rising action, climax, and falling action no longer holds, because this view also assumes the traditional concept of wholeness. Richard Schickel, writing in 1969 about Andy Warhol's movie *Lonesome Cowboys*, observed: "I left *Cowboys* 10 minutes before it was over, on the grounds that since it had no beginning and no middle it probably had no ending either." Obviously, the reviewer was operating on a different concept of wholeness from that of the director. In fact, the best of contemporary movies—particularly those popular among young people—do operate on different assumptions. A movie is no longer fiction translated into film. The film has become an art form in its own right, with its own principles of narration and characterization, its own techniques, and its own concept of what completeness is. Much of what is innovative in literature today suggests that writers are attempting to adapt cinematic techniques to writing. It is wholly possible that in the future films will be considered literature, just as drama from the time of the Renaissance on has gained the status of literature.

Point of View

One of the fascinating things about literature is to consider the action from the point of view of the narrator. Point of view is a less significant factor in drama than in fiction or poetry because in drama many points of view may be operating at the same time. Even though the author may be speaking through one of the characters, his is not ordinarily the only viewpoint represented.

In fiction and poetry, however, the voice of the narrator is of prime importance. That voice may not be the author's own. John Donne wrote a verse epistle entitled "Sappho to Philaenis." In the poem, he adopts the thoughts and point of view of Sappho. Sappho is a persona, a mask for the writer. Donne assumes the mask as readily as Shaw writes speeches for Eliza Doolittle in his play *Pygmalion*. Always basic to reading a poem, therefore, is considering who the speaker is, whether the speaker is identified with the author, and, if he is not, who he represents and what kind of speaker he is.

In far more intricate ways, the point of view in fiction determines what action can be narrated. If the author's point of view is omniscient, that is, if he assumes the role of all-knowingness, he can include whatever he chooses to include. But space does not usually allow the writer to penetrate and make clear the motives of all of the characters. He may therefore focus on several of the main ones. In the following passage from Thomas Hardy's *The Mayor of Casterbridge*, the author's omniscient point of view permits him to see the entire scene, to describe sounds both outdoors and indoors, to give close details of a woman's appearance, and to know the thoughts of another woman and her daughter:

> Other clocks struck eight from time to time—one gloomily from the gaol, another from the gable of an almshouse, with a preparative creak of machinery, more audible than the note of the bell; a row of tall, varnished case-clocks from the interior of a clockmaker's shop joined in one after another just as the shutters were enclosing them, like a row of actors delivering their final speeches before the fall of the curtain; then chimes were heard stammering out the Sicilian Mariners' Hymn; so that chronologists of the advanced school were appreciably on their way to the next hour before the whole business of the old one was satisfactorily wound up.
>
> In an open space before the church walked a woman with her gown-sleeves rolled up so high that the edge of her under-linen was visible, and her skirt tucked up through her pocket hole. She carried a loaf under her arm from which she was pulling pieces of bread, and handing them to some other women who walked with her; which pieces they nibbled critically. The sight reminded Mrs. Henchard-Newson and her daughter that they had an appetite; and they inquired of the woman for the nearest baker's.

In a somewhat different approach to narration, the author can voluntarily place limits upon his point of view and let one of the characters within the scene narrate. As an author, he therefore limits himself only to what the character can see and hear. In the following passage from *The Sound and the Fury*, Faulkner narrates from the point of view of the thirty-three-year-old idiot Benjy:

> Through the fence, between the curling flower spaces, I could see them hitting. They were coming toward where the flag was and I went along the fence. Luster was hunting in the grass by the flower tree. They took the flag out, and they were hitting. Then they put the flag back and they went to the table, and he hit and the other hit. Then they went on, and I went along the fence. Luster came away from the flower tree and we went along the fence and they stopped and we stopped and I looked through the fence while Luster was hunting in the grass.
>
> "Here, caddie." He hit. They went away across the pasture. I held to the fence and watched them going away.

Once an author chooses a limited point of view, any number of other options present themselves. He can turn over the narration to the main character of the story and let him relate his own story, or he can choose any other character involved in the story to narrate what he observes. Each change of focus, of course, holds the possibility of an entirely different kind of story because, obviously, no two people view the same situation in the same way. One of the fascinating demonstrations of a story told from a variety of points of view is Robert Browning's long narrative poem "The Ring and the Book." In ten of the twelve books composing this long poem, we read the contrasting views of different characters and groups concerning the story of Guido, Pompilia, and Caponsacchi. The reader is not finally given the author's definitive version; the truth is left to be interpreted as the reader wishes to view it through the character of his own choice.

Thus, the narrator may or may not be the author. If he is not the author, he may be identified closely with him or he may diverge sharply from the author's opinions, just as if he were an entirely different person. Only the investigation of point of view in terms of particular stories and poems can suggest the rich diversity that is open to the writer by this means.

SUGGESTIONS FOR WRITING ABOUT ACTION

Writing about action or plot depends on being able to answer questions like the following as they may apply to a particular story, play, or poem:

1. Why has the author selected certain details of action and not others which we may possibly know from another source, for example, from a different version of the same story by another author (various works based upon the Trojan war) or from actual experience (Truman Capote's *In Cold Blood*)? What actions does the writer fail to narrate that would affect the way we respond to the story? Where are the gaps? Why do particular actions seem to be omitted?
2. What is gained by the particular point of view the author chooses for his narration?
3. What particular effects of suspense, irony, or discovery are gained by the arrangement of the incidents, particularly if they depart from a straight chronological scheme? Why does the story begin or end as it does? What actions seem to be basically cinematic? In what way?
4. What significant changes occur in the course of the action that lend themselves to interpretation? In what way do changes in action act as clues to changes that occur in characters?
5. What elements of foreshadowing permit the reader to foresee the eventual outcome of the action?
6. Is more than one story operating at one and the same time in the same work (subplots)? Do various lines of action comment on one another? Do they reinforce one another, or do they contrast?
7. What characters or forces determine the action?
8. What are the key events in the narration? Why are these more important than others? What seemingly unimportant details of action take on special significance in terms of the writer's overall purpose?
9. Why are some events that may seem strange or improbable included in the action? How are events narrated that seem to deviate from the way we would normally expect them to happen?
10. In what way do actions shape and change characters?

Setting

Setting, of course, is closely associated with the staging of drama and with descriptive passages in fiction and poetry. In drama, the scene may be served by a simple backdrop and a few props or, even if these are dispensed with, as they frequently are in modern productions, it can be supplied by the imagination of the audience. But in either case, the physical properties creating a setting are not as important as the function of the scene in the mind of the writer and reader.

The Setting in Fiction

In Conrad's *Heart of Darkness*, the setting of the story is literal and vivid, but it is also a means for revealing the significance of the action. Each move that Marlow makes into the interior of the Belgian Congo of the nineteenth century seeking out Mr. Kurtz—a journey Conrad himself had taken in 1890—retraces the adventures of Kurtz's soul on this earth to its final state of deepest horror and savagery. A journey to another place would not have told the same story. Only the setting in Africa provides Conrad with the symbolic implications that he needs for this commentary upon mankind. In this story, as in many others, he describes a special world, a setting removed from the familiar scene and the usual trappings of civilization—a moral island, as it were—that tests man's essential values and capacities when he is released from the ordinary pressures of everyday life. The setting of a typical Conrad story is almost as restricted as a theatrical stage, and it must almost always be taken into account in speaking of the characters and the action.

In other fiction, of course, the setting may be a less integral part of the story than it is in *Heart of Darkness;* it may be provided only as if it were a landscape in the background. Modern writers, however, tend less often to treat the setting perfunctorily. The development of the social sciences in the twentieth century has placed strong emphasis on the total environment, including the actual place one lives; a corresponding school of realistic writers in the early twentieth century and thereafter devoted new attention to the influence of environment on their characters. Thus works like Sherwood Anderson's *Winesburg, Ohio,* Sinclair Lewis' *Main Street,* and James Farrell's *Studs Lonigan* are almost as much stories about places as they are about people.

In reading and writing about fiction, it is important first to dismiss the idea that description is only pictorial filler, that we can skip over it quickly to get on with what will happen next. Ironically, the same reader who would skip description might be aghast at the idea of buying a recording that included only the "great moments" of a symphony, only the melodies without any of the preparation, transitions, or development. Even though description may to some readers seem a delay in the action, it may very well be the part that helps them understand more fully what happens next and why it happens. When and where are inseparably tied in with who, what, and why.

The Setting in Drama

A setting in drama can be scenery against which the characters in a play move, or it can represent a more intangible, symbolic force, acting on the characters and reinforcing the thought of the play. The setting of Ibsen's *The Wild Duck,* for example, is conceived in symbolical terms, even though in an actual stage production the setting would demand nothing more than the usual accumulation of household furniture to suggest rooms in a house. Four of the five acts of the play take place in a combination studio-sitting room in the home of Hialmar Ekdal. Constantly referred to throughout the play, however, is an adjoining garret. A producer would have the option of making part of this garret visible to the audience, but he would not need to because Ibsen supplies all the necessary details about it in the dialogue.

Inside the garret are boxes to serve as nests for poultry, pigeons, rabbits, and a wounded wild duck that can no longer fly; four or five withered Christmas trees; a cupboard full of picture books; and a large clock that no longer runs. One of the characters says that the books belonged to an old sea captain, called "The Flying Dutchman," who used to live in the house.

All of the details and implications of the garret cannot be explored here, but the relationship of each of the main characters to the garret is a means of characterization in the play. Old Man Ekdal has come to think of the garret as a real world where he can hunt and putter about; the young girl Hedvig loves the wondrousness of the books and the otherworldliness of the room; Hialmar Ekdal, the girl's father, is constantly tempted to spend more time in the garret than at his photography in the studio. It is alternately a timeless world of illusion, romance, and escape. Some of the characters in the play prefer the garret to the studio; some never enter it; some stay outside but look in. All in all, Ibsen has translated the theme of reality and illusion that pervades the play into the very setting in which his characters move. The play cannot be fully understood without considering their actions in terms of the scene.

The Setting in Poetry

At a particularly breathtaking sight, people are often heard to say, "Words cannot describe such a scene." Yet poetry among the forms of literary expression often catches the quality of the indescribable; if often succeeds in conveying what the writer has seen and thought and felt. Reading the British poets from Chaucer to Thomas is to gain a knowledge of and familiarity with the English countryside that are second only to seeing it, and some of what they have seen in times past can no longer be seen. Descriptive poetry, however, is not merely scenic. It is often the point of departure for reflection, a typical pattern in Wordsworth's poems. The description cannot be dismissed as ornamentation. It is the source of the thought; it permits the reader to have some sense of the poet's experience. In "Lines Composed a Few Miles Above Tintern Abbey," Wordsworth first describes the scene, then comments:

> These beauteous forms,
> Through a long absence, have not been to me
> As is a landscape to a blind man's eye:
> But oft, in lonely rooms, and 'mid the din

Of towns and cities, I have owed to them,
In hours of weariness, sensations sweet,
Felt in the blood, and felt along the heart;
And passing even into my purer mind,
With tranquil restoration:—feelings too
Of unremembered pleasure: such, perhaps,
As have no slight or trivial influence
On that best portion of a good man's life,
His little, nameless, unremembered, acts
Of kindness and of love. Nor less, I trust,
To them I may have owed another gift,
Of aspect more sublime; that blessed mood,
In which the burthen of the mystery,
In which the heavy and the weary weight
Of all this unintelligible world,
Is lightened: . . .

The setting is the inspiration of the poem.

In other kinds of poems, more dramatic in quality, the description serves as a substitute for a stage. Often, however, the scene needs to be inferred, as in Archibald MacLeish's short poem "The End of the World":

Quite unexpectedly as Vasserot
The armless ambidextrian was lighting
A match between his great and second toe
And Ralph the lion was engaging in biting
The neck of Madame Sossman while the drum
Pointed, and Teeny was about to cough
In waltz-time swinging Jocko by the thumb—
Quite unexpectedly the top blew off:

And there, there overhead, there, there, hung over
Those thousands of white faces, those dazed eyes,
There in the starless dark the poise, the hover,
There with vast wings across the canceled skies,
There in the sudden blackness the black pall
Of nothing, nothing, nothing—nothing at all.

In this poem, the setting itself is a metaphor: the world is a circus, a variation upon those more familiar lines from Shakespeare:

All the world's a stage
And all the men and women merely players.

MacLeish again used the particular implications of the circus metaphor years later when he wrote his drama *J.B.*, based on the story of Job. In that play, all of the action takes place inside a circus tent—a kind of total universe that includes man and God.

In a poem entitled "Come Up from the Fields Father," Whitman describes the reactions of a family to a letter carrying word that the only son has been gravely wounded in the war. The poem begins with the lines:

> Come up from the fields father, here's a letter from our Pete,
> And come to the front door mother, here's a letter from thy dear son.

After this brief stanza with its sense of foreboding, the narrative shifts to describe the setting, but the reader learns almost immediately that Whitman is providing more than a physical setting—he is describing an emotional setting for the news that will arrive:

> Lo, 'tis autumn,
> Lo, where the trees, deeper green, yellower and redder,
> Cool and sweeten Ohio's villages with leaves fluttering in the moderate
>   wind,
> Where apples ripe in the orchards hang and grapes on the trellis'd
>   vines,
> (Smell you the smell of the grapes on the vines?
> Smell you the buckwheat where the bees were lately buzzing?)
> Above all, lo, the sky so calm, so transparent after the rain, and with
>   wondrous clouds,
> Below too, all calm, all vital and beautiful, and the farm prospers well.

Into this world of calm and sensuous delicacy, the harsh news of the outside world comes as a stroke of lightning. Thereafter, we read of trembling and grief and, finally, death. The contrast the poet provides serves to intensify the feeling.

The Time of the Setting

A setting does not necessarily need to be current to seem familiar, nor do we necessarily need special historical knowledge about the past to appreciate a particular scene. Past and present have a remarkable way of fusing in the imagination, and any anachronisms there may be do not disturb us much. Writers have characteristically looked to the past to seek out parallels to the modern scene. Getting readers to involve themselves in the past is a device to detach them from immediate concerns, even though they know that the author is commenting on current problems. We are often willingly led by literature to consider what we would otherwise reject if it were treated directly. Giraudoux's *Tiger at the Gates*, for instance, is set in ancient Troy. The war between the Greeks and Trojans serves as a background for the dialogue. The play continues to enjoy revivals, some in modern dress, not because it retells an old story, but because it has become a perennial commentary on the theme of man and warfare. Yet the play was written by a man who was a member of the French government and, at the time of its production, it had special relevance to the situation in France in 1935. The scene of Giraudoux's play is a strategy that actually aids the reader in gaining a perspective on current turmoil. Of course, writers of stories, novels, and poems utilize the same technique. The revival of the past is a constant reminder not only that there is nothing new in human affairs, but also that the past holds infinite wisdom for the future.

SUGGESTIONS FOR WRITING ABOUT SETTING

To give a few examples of the uses of setting in literary works is only to suggest in this short discussion the kind of thought and emotional impact setting can convey, not to explore the full range of possibilities. The reader needs first to be aware of setting, then to look at details. These offer him an opportunity to interpret. For instance, there is Melville's use of a high brick wall in "Bartleby the Scrivener" to objectify the barrier within Bartleby's mind. And there is Chekhov's use of the barren cherry trees in his play *The Cherry Orchard* to comment, not without irony, on the changing social and political scene in Russia of the early twentieth century. These are all imaginative means of involving the reader in a concrete experience, tied to a place and time, and valuable clues to the thought of the literature.

Writing about setting should include enough description to make the reader familiar with details of the scene. These need not be quoted; they can be paraphrased and abbreviated. The next and more important step, then, is to say in what way the setting functions in the literary work. Questions of the following kind will provide guides for the reader:

1. In a play, how much detail do the stage directions give in describing the setting? Is the playwright explicit, or does he leave the scene to be interpreted in various ways by scene designer and stage director? Can you also supply an interpretation? In what way could the play be staged meaningfully?
2. If stage directions are sparse, to what extent can the setting be reconstructed from the dialogue? What are the essential props?
3. In a story or play, to what extent is the setting literally realistic or symbolical? If it is symbolical, in what way does the setting function? What clues does the writer give?
4. In a literary work, in what way does the setting relate significantly to the action? Are the two working together? Do they clash?
5. In what way does a character's response to the setting reveal things about him?
6. In what way is the setting a reinforcement of the theme of the work?
7. Particularly in poems, is the setting the point of departure for the thought or emotion expressed? Does it serve as contrast? Does

the description supply commentary on the author or the speaker in the poem?

8. How is description narrated? Who is telling what he sees and what is happening? What difference does the point of view make in the nature of the description? What methods of description are used? Does the writer depend on precise details, lyrical suggestion, comparisons, and allusions? What is the effect on you?

9. If the scene is remote in time or place, what correspondences can be found in the details of setting and situation that will permit you to draw parallels between the past and the present? How contemporaneous is the setting?

10. To what extent do elements of nature or of the environment become active forces in the literary work, changing the action and determining the fate of characters?

5

Form and Structure

There is no question of the need for structure in the useful arts as opposed to the fine arts. An engineer who builds a bridge has to work with a design first and then with actual structural plans. In like manner, an architect works both with external shape and interior arrangement. Though the function of form and structure in literature is not as readily apparent as it is in construction, it is not less basic to the art. The principles may be less mechanical, but they are no less functional in making a literary work what it is.

Because the external appearance of a literary work is one of the first ways to classify it as fiction, drama, or poetry, form must be discussed in terms of each of the genres, not as a general principle common to all. Further, of the various elements that concern the reader of literature, form is perhaps the most technical. The more knowledge you have of structural matters, the more aware you will be of the way form is operating to shape the literary work and increase its readability. But a brief discussion can't make professionals out of general readers. So we will consider here those matters of form and structure that are readily observable to the nonprofessional and can aid your understanding and appreciation of literature if you are more conscious of them. Sean O'Faolain, himself an accomplished short story writer, speaks of the short story as showing the "most highly perfected technique in prose-fiction" and emphasizes that we read these stories not alone for what they say but "for the joy we get out of seeing a craftsman doing a delicate job of work." Every reader should have some awareness of how a writer does his job.

Tradition and Experiment in Fiction

The novel and the short story are perhaps the least formally structured of the various kinds of literary works that are produced; that is, fiction seems to be less bound by set conventional forms than drama or poetry. Drama is linked to the theater and poetry to recitation—at least in times past—but fiction continues to be a form designed mainly to be read silently from the printed page. Characteristically, it is written in prose, and its appearance on the page is fairly uniform. Long works are divided into chapters or sections. In such relatively superficial matters, most novels are alike; but, as far as the form of the novel is concerned, there is no designated length, no set number of parts or divisions. One might note that some experiments in fiction often hinge on trying to make the external appearance of the printed page look different, thus trying for new effects. An early experimental novel like Dos Passos' *The 42nd Parallel* included newspaper headlines and biographical sketches, so that the novel took on a multigenre effect similar to what we now familiarly experience as a multimedia effect. A recent experimental work, *Informed Sources* by Willard Bain, is called a novel, but its typography sometimes resembles verse, sometimes cartoonlike designs, often with symbols and single letters splashed on the page instead of words. Attempts such as these are designed to break down the deadening effects of habit in readers so that their customary assumptions about fiction are challenged. Readers have the option of trying to come to grips with a new approach, figuring out what serious purpose it may have, or of dismissing it as mere foolishness. Experiments always meet with detractors because the familiar is pleasant and comforting. Works that alter patterns are disturbing.

Internal Structure of Fiction

Basic to understanding structure in fiction is coming to a realization that it can be thought about in several ways. The concept of structure does not have to be limited to the most apparent one of putting parts together in an orderly way. That is one concept, but it is essentially a static notion to think of a literary work as if it were a construction. It conjures up an image of a novelist building his work as if he were a carpenter or mason and, when everything is complete, we as readers look upon his workmanship.

Literary structure, however, can also be thought of in more active terms, not so much as an assemblage of parts according to a blueprint but as an ongoing process in which characters interact and ideas, images, and themes recur and connect. A novel is most conveniently thought of as a developing form, as finding a shape as the writer writes. Actually, even if a writer chooses to imitate another author's form, he can do it only in the more obvious ways of using structural techniques another writer has used, like Faulkner's choice in *The Sound and the Fury* of four different narrators in four sections focused on four days in the history of the Compson family or Melville's miniature encyclopedia on whales in the chapter on cetology in *Moby Dick*. But the fact remains that novels do not have set forms that can be labeled and followed exactly. The terms that are used refer to specific techniques or general approaches. Thus, an epistolary novel is one like Samuel Richardson's *Pamela* that uses the letter as its chief device of revealing the characters and their story. A picaresque novel is one like Fielding's *Tom Jones* that uses a series of rambling episodes as a means of taking its rogue hero through adventures that comment on everyday life. But these are essentially structural patterns in very broad terms; they can assume many different forms in the hands of different writers. For purposes of writing about form in fiction, four structural features are worthy of attention: time structure, space structure, character patterns, and motifs.

Time Structure

Every novelist and short story writer has to come to terms with chronology. Given a set of circumstances that represent his story, where does he begin? If he begins his story at the culmination of events, then he transfers the attention of the reader from a concern with what will happen to a concern with how it happened and why it happened. A shift in time structure can change the primary emphasis of a story from plot to character because if the outline of the events is known in advance, then interest focuses on the way characters respond to those happenings. And if time is not a central structural feature of a story, the major emphasis then falls on theme or image.

Time structure obviously affects the dramatic impact of the narration. Always decisive to a particular effect is the reader's knowledge about the characters and events. If the reader knows the outcome in advance, his attention can be drawn to the ironies of circumstance because at any point in the story it is possible for the reader to know through the narrator what a character himself cannot know about his future. Rearrangement of time, therefore, can move the reader to emotional concerns about the characters that would not otherwise be possible in a straight chronological sequence. In addition to the actual chronology of events, there is also the matter of timing in a story, which is in part structural and in part stylistic. It concerns the time at which the narrator chooses to reveal details about his characters, particularly about their past. It is one technique to begin a story at the beginning and move to the end. It is another to start at a given point and then with calculation to reveal what only needs to be known at any particular time. In Fitzgerald's "Babylon Revisited," we are first told that Charles Wales has returned to Paris where he once spent a wild two years with his wife Helen. Then we learn that he is returning to visit his daughter Honoria, who is living under the legal guardianship of his sister-in-law Marion. These are all current circumstances in the story. Details of the past begin to unfold. We learn that Helen, his wife, is dead and only later in the story that she died of a heart attack and still later that Charles had locked Helen out of the house during a snowstorm. Each of these details moves the story back in time and helps to explain the conflict between him and Marion and the reason she will probably not release Honoria again to her father. This structuring of the action clearly becomes a matter of interest in itself and affects the entire pace and emphasis of the story.

Space Structure

Space structure refers simply to the geographical bounds a writer limits himself to. The choice of location is usually closely allied with the time element, and the two affect the scope of the story. If a story has only one location and a brief time span, then the writer usually treats only a fairly limited set of circumstances, just as a dramatist has to adapt his action to a particular stage setting. Nevertheless, it should be added that an author can always employ narrative devices like the flashback, the interior monologue, the dream, or the vision, which will carry the story beyond its immediate geographical dimensions.

One of the remarkable things about James Joyce in *Ulysses* is that he manages to compress the epic dimensions of Homer's *Odyssey*, the model for his characters and their relationships, into a twenty-four-hour period in Dublin. In linear sequence, from the time of Odysseus' departure from home to his return, Homer's epic ranges to distant places over a period of twenty years. Joyce's reduced space and time structure has altered the effect of the original completely and placed demands on the author to achieve the scope and complexity that he does by a variety of narrative techniques. What is most obvious is that Joyce's novel is no longer a tale of adventure as Homer's epic is; *Ulysses* is a psychological exploration.

Writing about time and space structure mainly involves two things: (1) deciphering and describing it if it is sufficiently complex, as in Faulkner's "Barn Burning," and (2) discussing the effects gained by the choices the author has made. Fitzgerald's "Babylon Revisited," already discussed briefly above, treats two Parises: Paris, the Babylon-like city of young Charles Wales's two-year binge and the Paris of the immediate present of the story, seemingly tame, empty, and provincial. This contrast simply reflects the way the new Charles see things and thus becomes a means also of revealing changes that have taken place in him. We see that the elements of literature are never independent of one another, but that the who, what, where, when, how, and why combine to create the organic structure of the literary work.

Character Patterns

Thinking of characters in terms of structure will often reveal that they fall into groupings which reinforce the theme of the story. The division may be as simple as that between characters who are good and those who are evil, particularly in stories like Hawthorne's, which are strongly allegorical. In other instances, the interrelationships may be more involved. To illustrate again from "Babylon Revisited." There are six main characters in Fitzgerald's story. The protagonist is Charles Wales, eager to gain possession of his daughter Honoria, who in turn is anxious to live with her father. They represent one group. Charles's attempt to establish this relationship permanently is the object of the action. Marion, the sister-in-law, is Charles's antagonist; she resists his effort to regain Honoria. Although her husband Lincoln is not wholly unsympathetic toward Charles, he stands by his wife and therefore represents with her a second group of characters who will determine the future of the first group. The remaining two characters are "sudden ghosts out of the past"—Duncan Schaeffer and Lorraine Quarrles. They are carry-overs from Charles's earlier experience in Paris. When they intrude into the household of Marion and Lincoln, all six characters for the first time are brought face to face with one another. It is a decisive scene in the story, and the result is that Charles's hopes to have Honoria are frustrated. The characters are forced into two groups of three. Charles is associated with Duncan and Lorraine, whether he chooses to be or not; under the circumstances, Honoria is forced to remain with her aunt and uncle. Father and daughter are together only for the duration of the story.

In a similar kind of analysis, examination of character patterns in other works can sometimes provide a means for writing about the story that might not otherwise be possible if the characters are viewed only one at a time.

Motifs

Motifs are an expressive means of repeating the same idea a number of times throughout the story. Motifs are structural in the sense that they connect parts of the story by taking the reader back to an earlier scene or reminding him of a constant feature about a character which remains unchanged. Fitzgerald's "Babylon Revisited" again serves as an apt illustration, indicating, of course, that a single short story depends on any number of structural features.

The story opens in the Ritz bar in Paris. Charles Wales has a drink. When the barman asks him if he wants another drink, he refuses, saying that he is "going slow these days"—a reminder of the days when he was "going pretty strong." Charles later explains that he has vowed to have only one drink every afternoon. In the story, his daily whiskey becomes a motif, indicating Charles's determination not to fall back into old excesses. At the end of the story when Charles is again in the Ritz bar after he has learned that he will not be able to regain the custody of his daughter, the narrator might have indicated a change in Charles by having him take a second drink. But the motif is not broken. As the story closes, Charles once more shakes his head as the barman looks questioningly at his empty glass. It is a final touch in the story that confirms the reader's sympathies for Charles.

There is nothing particularly subtle about Fitzgerald's use of this motif. Each time it occurs the reader is fully aware that it is a test of character which Charles has set for himself and has to pass. Yet the motif also adds suspense and connective purpose to the story as a whole. Recurring themes, actions, and symbols are therefore important clues both to the meaning of the story and to its organic unity.

Freedom and Convention in Dramatic Structure

The matter of dramatic structure is so closely linked to the history of the stage and the playhouse that the one can hardly be explained except in terms of the other. Further, the active presence of the audience viewing live performances has an additional effect on the structure of the play. Act divisions which provide a rest for the performers, an intermission for the audience, and an opportunity to reset the stage are the formal solutions to the time and space problems of drama. Even long movies now provide an intermission for the audience, although the break seems to have affected the structure of movies very little as yet; it is merely an interruption of the running of the film at an appropriate halfway point—a matter of stopping the projector rather than a formal division of the action into two parts.

In plays, however, act and scene divisions have very specific effects on the structure of a play because playwrights characteristically seem concerned with drawing the audience back into the theater after each break. Thus, two-, three-, four-, and five-act plays tend to break down into discrete and self-contained parts. The effect is different from a one-act play with multiple scenes which have the continuousness of a movie. The kind of theater for which an author writes also frequently determines the structure of a play.

Dramatic Structure and the Theater

Greek tragedies, which were produced in open-air amphitheaters with little scenery, belong to the tradition of continuous-action plays. The setting did not change. The scene divisions used in printed versions of the plays today marked the coming or going of one of the two or three actors who were available to play a larger number of roles. And scene divisions were also influenced by the role of the chorus, a conventional feature of the theater of that day. Even though Greek plays are not divided into acts, many of them fall into five formal divisions: prologos, parados, epeisodion, stasimon, and exodos. These are determined to a large extent by the entrance, function, and exit of the chorus. Playwrights therefore observed fairly rigid dramatic conventions in a theater which might have been used far more flexibly, as indeed it was on the Elizabethan stage.

The open-air Elizabethan theater, epitomized by the Globe Playhouse, provided at least three main acting areas. The projected platform, the rear stage with a curtain, and the upper stage, which was also provided with a curtain, were all adaptable to different purposes. The characters of the play could act as if they moved from outside to inside, or from place to place, by shifting their location on the stage or by describing the scene in the poetry of their lines. Properties and machinery were used to suggest localities, but the theater was not primarily devoted, as later theaters were, to creating an illusion of reality. The scenes could shift rapidly, and an entire play might be produced in two and one-half or three hours, broken only by convenient musical intermissions for the benefit of the actors and the audience.

Thus, to produce Shakespeare's plays today with the same effectiveness as they were in the Elizabethan theaters demands an equally adaptable stage or a vehicle as flexible as film. Actually, the act and scene divisions in texts of Shakespeare's plays are additions of early editors. The structure of these plays was influenced by the stage itself, not by arbitrary conventions, as in Greek times.

Neoclassical drama of the seventeenth century in France, however, was bound strictly by rules. Playwrights like Corneille and Racine wrote plays in an effort to observe what critics of that time had established as the dramatic unities. The unities limited a play to a single line of action in one place within a twenty-four-hour period. These principles were inferred from Aristotle's *Poetics,* based on observations of plays being produced in Athens in the fifth century B.C., but presumably no Greek dramatist ever considered himself as formally bound to the unwritten unities as the dramatists of the distant future were in their attempts to imitate them. Greek dramatists observed conventions which the theater demanded; they did not have Aristotle as their mentor. Ironically, one of the purest examples of Greek tragedy in the neoclassical sense in John Milton's *Samson Agonistes* (1671), declared by Milton not to have been written for the stage at all.

Despite their differences, Greek and Roman plays, Elizabethan plays, and neoclassical plays are all strongly theatrical; that is, they do not deny the fact of the theater itself, that action takes place on a stage. They do not pretend to present an illusion of life itself. The proscenium-arch theater from 1660 on popularized the concept of illusionism. Elaborate scenery and fixed properties were designed to disguise the stage and transform it into the world of the play. Thus no longer would it have been possible for a Shakespeare of that day to write the forty-two scenes which make up *Antony and Cleopatra,* and Shakespeare's plays themselves were actually cut and adapted to be performed on a far less flexible stage. Drama settled into a conventional act structure, which was to dominate dramatic production until new concepts of staging in the twentieth century once again gave to dramatists a complete freedom of form.

What this brief survey of the influence of the stage and convention on dramatic structure suggests is that uniform standards of evaluation about form cannot be applied to all plays. One reader may prefer the economical structure of a Greek play; another, the range of an Elizabethan drama; another, the disciplined unity of a neoclassical drama; and still another, the loose fragmentary quality of many contemporary plays. But without reference to stage history, the final test of the form of a play, at least from the viewpoint of a reader, is its suitability to the dramatist's theme and purpose. Dramatists in this century who have attempted to say new things in new ways and, in particular, have attempted to depict inner actions as well as outer actions have had to seek new structures. Thus, Arthur Miller explains that certain scenes in *Death of a Salesman* are not flashbacks in time but are the past flowing into the present through the mind of Willy Loman. The structure of the play accommodates scenes of this kind because, as Miller describes it, the stage can be adapted either to the world of the moment or to the world of reverie. The fact remains, however, that a drama is not as flexible a form as the novel for purposes of psychological probing. Even though drama has found ways of escaping the immediate stage scene, the form still demands that a character's inner experiences be objectified. Thus in *Death of a Salesman*, Ben, who occupies Willy's thoughts, actually appears on the stage. This is memory objectified. It works as a device in this particular play, but having to show thought places far greater demands on the playwright than telling about it does on the writer of fiction.

Internal Structure of Drama

Basically, the setting of a play and its time divisions determine the external form of a play. Its internal structure, like fiction, depends on motifs of action, characters, themes, and symbols which run throughout the play as a whole and bridge what may be its leaps in time and place.

Chekhov's plays, for example, depend heavily on internal structure. Externally, his longer plays, all written in four acts, show the strong influence of Greek drama. They have a compactness which is reinforced by a limited setting, a limited span of time, and limited action. Typically, the main action occurs offstage; the onstage action concerns the indirect effects of those offstage occurrences on the characters. Thus, in *The Cherry Orchard*, the important action is the sale of the orchard. It is the major concern of the characters throughout the play, but the auction itself finally takes place between Acts II and III. At the end of Act III, when Lopahin announces that he has purchased the orchard, the play reaches its climax. The final act reflects not only the changes that will take place in the estate but those that will occur in the lives of these people.

Throughout Chekhov's play, the cherry orchard itself is the pervading symbol, and the characters may be classified by their attitudes toward it. They belong either to the old order of Russian society which would seek to preserve the beauty of the trees or to the new order which would chop them down to make the land useful for subdividing and building. Thus the characters fall into loose patterns in relation to the main symbol of the play.

The recurring motifs—the ominous sound of a breaking harp string, Madame Ranevsky's carelessness with money, the weeping, and mournful music—are important structural features of a play of this nature, because the dialogue is often marked by incoherence. Each character seems primarily dedicated to himself, thinking his own thoughts, and speaking little monologues. Not much communication takes place in a Chekov play in the sense of one character talking and responding to another; the dialogue does not build upon an idea, as a Shaw play does, for example. Chekhov's dialogue shapes an impression, not an argument, and the motifs are in part responsible for creating that illusive, mysterious quality that often pervades his plays.

The Range of Poetic Structure

Just as the novel seems better suited than the drama for subjects of broad scope and those of psychological depth, so the poem among the three genres seems best suited for subjects of small dimension and intimate feeling. Even though long poems on epic themes have been written, these tend to be versified dramas and narratives and vary considerably in effect from the lyric poem. Long poems are developed freely, in most instances limited only by a particular metric line but not by the kinds of stanza forms the lyric poet follows or imposes upon himself. The obvious exceptions to this statement are Dante's *Divine Comedy*, written in an interlocking rhyme pattern (*aba, bcb, cdc*), called terza rima, and Spenser's *The Faerie Queene*, written entirely in nine-line stanzas with a set rhyme scheme.

Set Forms of Poetry

As soon as a poet chooses to write in a set form, the form itself exercises a control over the content, not only limiting its range but shaping it as well. The best example is the sonnet, a fourteen-

line form with a set line length and rhyme scheme. The fourteen
lines of a sonnet limit the expression to a narrow range. "Narrow"
in this instance does not mean that sonnets are less profound or
less complex or that they have fewer implications than other poems,
but that they merely are less expansive. Whatever thought and feeling the poet has must be compressed into that space. Sonnet writing
is a severe discipline.

Within the bounds of the sonnet, two rhyme patterns have become traditional: the Shakespearean and the Petrarchan. The
first divides the fourteen lines into three groups of four lines and
one of two lines: *abab cdcd efef gg*. The Italian form divides the
fourteen lines into one group of eight lines and one group of six
lines: *abba abba cdc dcd,* although the rhyme schemes in both the
octave and sestet vary greatly. The effect of these divisions is
that the logic of the poem is affected by the form itself. In the
Shakespearean sonnet, the final couplet is always a break from the
previous twelve lines, and the twelve lines may break down into four
very precise logical units, as they do in Shakespeare's Sonnet 30:

> When to the sessions of sweet silent thought
> I summon up remembrance of things past.
> I sigh the lack of many a thing I sought
> And with old woes new wail my dear time's waste.
> Then can I drown an eye (unus'd to flow)
> For precious friends hid in death's dateless night,
> And weep afresh love's long since cancell'd woe,
> And moan th' expense of many a vanish'd sight.
> Then can I grieve at grievances foregone,
> And heavily from woe to woe tell o'er
> The sad account of fore-bemoaned moan,
> Which I new pay as if not paid before.
>   But if the while I think on thee, dear friend,
>   All losses are restor'd and sorrows end.

In this poem, the parts are introduced by the key connective words
"When ... Then ... Then ... But." These four words also shape the
logic. The poem consists of three variations on a single theme with
a final conclusion.

The Italian form achieves a different effect, illustrated by Wordsworth's sonnet to John Milton, given the title "London, 1802":

> Milton! thou shouldst be living at this hour:
> England hath need of thee: she is a fen
> Of stagnant waters: altar, sword, and pen,
> Fireside, the heroic wealth of hall and bower,
> Have forfeited their ancient English dower
> Of inward happiness. We are selfish men;
> Oh! raise us up, return to us again;
> And give us manners, virtue, freedom, power.

Thy soul was like a Star, and dwelt apart;
Thou hadst a voice whose sound was like the sea:
Pure as the naked heavens, majestic, free,
So didst thou travel on life's common way,
In cheerful godliness; and yet thy heart
The lowliest duties on herself did lay.

After a brief opening invocation, the poem describes conditions in England that Wordsworth deplores. A break comes after line eight. The final six lines, then, give reasons why a man of Milton's character and spirit might again be able to help. The thought is conveniently accommodated to the form. (For discussion of other stanza forms and meter, see the Glossary under Stanza and Versification.)

The Effect of the Medium

Perhaps in none of the other genres does the form influence the reader as forcefully as it does in the poem. The medium has its own effect quite apart from the content—or if not "quite apart" from the content, then in conjunction with it. But the form has its own message. The sonnet speaks preciseness, logicality, and compactness. The closed couplet of two rhyming lines speaks pithiness and certainty. The limerick speaks bounciness and light-heartedness. The poet's feeling for form undoubtedly influences his choice in the first place, with the result that content and form fuse in such a way that the "message" of the form reinforces the thought of the poem.

The Paradox of Form

The paradox of self-imposed form lies in the fact that control has the capacity to free expression, not inhibit it. The imagination must find ways to circumvent the restraints of form. Form encourages invention. Poetic creation is the act of making concrete the highly intangible images and sensations of the imagination. It is an act of ordering and channeling thoughts and feelings.

In an interview, Edward Villella, a distinguished ballet dancer, once referred to this paradoxical effect of form and discipline. He spoke of the highly structured nature of most ballet, the way in which each step is prescribed, and the disciplined technique necessary to perform the movements. Yet he added that when he was most in control of his technique he had the greatest experience of absolute freedom, as if he were floating on air. One might observe that an audience also has the same liberating reaction when the artist is in full control. If he has to struggle or force himself, then the audience becomes conscious of the form and technique itself, not the total experience and expression. In a similar way, form aids the poet. A parachute in the open sky is not a burden. It is the only safe way down.

Free Forms: Rhetorical Structure

Free verse forms do not imply an absence of form, only a greater flexibility and a greater dependence on internal structural features. One of these forms, blank verse, which is unrhymed lines of iambic pentameter, must be considered one of the more flexible forms a poet can use. It is adaptable to almost any subject of any scope. Milton wrote his vast epics *Paradise Lost* and *Paradise Regained* in blank verse; Robert Frost wrote an intimate and homey poem, "Mending Wall," in the same meter.

Free verse as a form abandons rhyme schemes, set stanzaic patterns, and regular line lengths, but it cannot escape rhythmic design, controlling images, repetitions, and a variety of rhetorical strategies which bind the parts together. Walt Whitman, who sought freedom from traditional forms and expressed themes of freedom in his poetry, was yet highly susceptible to structural patterns. His short poem "I Hear America Singing" illustrates his strong tendencies toward repetition, parallel structure, rhythmic balance, contrast, and the sustained image:

> I hear America singing, the varied carols I hear,
> Those of mechanics, each one singing his as it should be blithe and
>   strong,
> The carpenter singing his as he measures his plank or beam,
> The mason singing his as he makes ready for work, or leaves off work,
> The boatman singing what belongs to him in his boat, the deckhand
>   singing on the steamboat deck,
> The shoemaker singing as he sits on his bench, the hatter singing as
>   he stands,
> The wood-cutter's song, the ploughboy's on his way in the morning, or
>   at noon intermission or at sundown,
> The delicious singing of the mother, or of the young wife at work, or of
>   the girl sewing or washing,
> Each singing what belongs to him or her and to none else,
> The day what belongs to the day—at night the party of young fellows,
>   robust, friendly,
> Singing with open mouths their strong melodious songs.

In its irregularities, Whitman's poem seeks its own structures. Free verse represents only a different concept of what form can be.

Since Whitman's time, of course, free verse forms have become more and more common, but the popularity of free verse does not deny the importance of structure. Contemporary poetry simply confirms that the poet, with his typical inventiveness, constantly finds new ways to shape poems. After all, the imaginative fusion of words into form is the quality that continues to give poetry its uniqueness among the various modes of literary expression. (For additional discussion, see the Glossary under Anaphora, Free Verse, Imagism, and Sound Effects.)

SUGGESTIONS FOR WRITING ABOUT FORM

Writing about form depends, first, on a perception of what form is doing in a particular literary work. It further requires a special way of looking in order to see what the structural basis of a composition is. One significant contribution of the cubist painters to our way of looking at things was their idea that everything is a composite of shapes and designs. Their technique demonstrated this idea; paintings emerged as combinations of triangles, rectangles, and circles. This technique helped others to see what the cubists themselves perceived with a keener eye.

Writing about structure must attempt also to demonstrate what you intuit about form. But vague generalizations are of no help. The demonstration must finally be reduced to hard facts—counting the parts, determining why the divisions are made as they are, seeking out the less obvious connectives, recognizing patterns, determining the way themes and motifs shape the whole, and finally verbalizing what the total effects are.

Questions like the following suggest possible leads for discussion of matters of form:

1. What is the total effect of the work's structure? Does it seem to be a continuum? Is it a combination of fragments? Does the whole fall into an orderly sequence of parts?
2. What is the significance of the parts? At what point is a division made? Why? What effect would be altered if the division had not occurred?
3. Besides identifying the main parts of a work, what patterns emerge either through characters, symbols, motifs, or ideas? Can characters be grouped? Do the groupings shed light on the relationships between characters? Is there any character who does not seem to fit any group? If so, what does that signify?
4. What are the time arrangement and space dimensions of the work? If the author severely limits these, do they work to advantage? What effect is gained?

5. In what way is time treated? Is there a straight chronological scheme? A reversal? What is the purpose of any alteration of the time scheme? What effects would be lost if the time and space plan were changed?
6. What is the particular suitability of the form to the themes and ideas of the work itself? How does the form support the content?
7. Does the choice of form in any way run contrary to the content of the work, so that the form is ironic or satiric? Are all subjects appropriate to every form? Do jingles express profundities? Can an inappropriate form for a particular subject be a way to mock it?
8. In what way can the form of the work as a whole be characterized? What is the "message of the medium"?
9. In what way can form be the most important part of the work? (Reconsider John Nist's poem "Revolution: The Vicious Circle" on p. 13.) Why are words arranged as they are (as in a Cummings poem)?
10. In what way is the language itself acting as a structural feature, particularly in a poem? What are the grammatical patterns? The rhetorical patterns? The metric patterns? The rhyme scheme? How are they working together?

6

Language, Symbol, and Imagery

A writer's passion for language is often his incentive for writing. Words crystallize his thoughts, realize his emotions, and bring the images of his mind to the life of literature. The vitality, the imaginativeness, the beauty of this creation depend on words.

In one sense, the concerns of the imaginative writer are not far different from those of any other writer, whether he is an amateur or a professional. He needs to have an adequate stock of words to begin with. He has to be concerned with their meanings, both the accuracy of their literal use and their extended implications. He has to be concerned with the fact that language grows out of a variety of contexts which relate to age, occupation, education, ethnic background, social status, and a host of other factors, and that words derive associations from all of these sources. He has to be concerned with the interaction of words in any particular verbal context—what I. A. Richards calls the "interinanimation of words"—because in context the words gain a tone and meaning all their own. Words are the writer's paints, and every writer must show some capacity to use their coloration, texture, intensity, and harmony to produce an identifiable style.

Ultimately, however, there is always the distinction between the dabbler and the artist. The concerns of the literary artist characteristically do go beyond those of the ordinary writer in his desire to tap the powers of language to communicate his imaginative vision and his search for ways to push the limits of language outward in order to express the inexpressible. Because imaginative literature often accomplishes these ends, we look to it as the highest expression of man's capacity with language.

Metaphorical Language

Metaphorical or figurative language is perhaps the writer's most important single source of imaginative power. It almost always represents the writer's invasion of an alien verbal context to bring back a word or phrase or image to work into a different setting of words. Metaphorical language defies ordinary associations; it makes fresh ones by seeking out likenesses in dissimilar areas of experience.

Metaphor is possible only because our common experiences lead us to use words in familiar patterns. Words cluster around topics; certain words fit together. Thus, phrases like these are totally familiar and factual:

He was born.
He served in the air force during the war.
He was a turret gunner on a plane.
He was killed during an attack on the enemy.

Randall Jarrell's short poem "The Death of the Ball Turret Gunner," however, shows what a complete transformation can take place when these prosaic phrases are translated into metaphorical language:

From my mother's sleep I fell into the State,
And I hunched in its belly till my wet fur froze.
Six miles from earth, loosed from its dream of life,
I woke to black flak and the nightmare fighters.
When I died they washed me out of the turret with a hose.

What Jarrell has added is a whole new set of associations which go beyond the simple facts of being born, fighting, and dying; these additions can be suggested by phrases such as these:

Being in the womb is like sleeping.
The rapid time between birth and army service is like a fall.
The plane is the State.
The ball turret is the plane's belly.
Being in the turret is like being in the womb.
In his furry suit, he is like an animal.

Life on earth is living in a dream.
Flying high is like being released from something.
The attack is a nightmare.
Dying is an awakening.
His bodily remains are like debris.

These paraphrases of the metaphors are not an interpretation of
the poem, but they do reveal what areas of experience the poet has
explored to bring imaginativeness and feeling to the basic experience and to make a shocking commentary upon the life
and death of a young man. Further, only metaphorical language
makes possible the compression that the poem achieves and the
intensity that grows out of that telescoping of language. The
metaphors add the feeling; the metaphors invite the extensions of
meaning. They are the source of the poetry.

The one sustained metaphor of Randall Jarrell's short poem is
that of sleeping and waking. Living is sleeping; dying is waking.
In fact, the "I" of the poem is awake, telling his experience; only he
is dead. The poem therefore turns upon a paradox. We ordinarily
think of living as waking; death is like a kind of sleep, a comparison invited by the appearance of the body in sleep and in
death. The effective metaphor, however, does not always depend
upon the obvious likeness but frequently upon the unexpected
similarity, even though the poet might find only one possible link
between two verbal contexts. In "A Valediction: Forbidding
Mourning," John Donne compares separated lovers to the legs of
a compass hinged together at the top. In a sustained metaphor,
he relates the movements of the compass to the movements and
emotions of the lovers. It is the kind of ingenious conceit that
prompted Dr. Johnson to condemn the Metaphysical poets of the
seventeenth century when he said that they yoked "the most
heterogeneous ideas . . . by violence together."

The effect of a metaphor, of course, does not depend on
its ingeniousness but mainly on its concreteness and meaningful-
ness. As a comparison, the purpose of metaphor is to clarify, not
to cloud the thought. If it draws on a subject or experience that
is totally unfamiliar to most readers, it cannot succeed in il-
luminating the thought. If it draws on that which is too familiar,
it also fails because the reader does not respond to the overused
metaphor. Nor does he ordinarily recognize the dead metaphors
which are the common stock of our daily speech—"the hand of a
clock," "the foot of a mountain," "to be keyed up," or "a tubby man."
A reexamination of any page of our own writing will reveal the extent to which metaphor is a natural way of thinking. The artist

goes further to depend on it as a major means of conveying his perceptions.

Symbolic Language

Like metaphor, symbol-making is a natural process. It is a way of simplifying the complexities of thought and experience by hitting upon one thing as representative of many. The symbol may be used as a reminder, a signal, a call to action. It is a means by which men seek to express the unity of their perceptions and experiences. It is a hook to hang on to.

In 1969, the "closed fist" became the symbol of a whole movement of defiance and protest among militant Blacks. It was a symbol that could be dramatized, pictured, and spoken. Even though the symbol had special implications for that particular movement, it was basically a borrowing of a universal symbol. We have always recognized the clenched fist as a symbol of threat and resistance, just as we tend to recognize doves as symbols of peace, the crown as a symbol of authority, and water as a symbol of purification. Symbols such as these which have become traditional are called universal symbols. Literature draws heavily on them, but it also creates occasional symbols, like the duck in Ibsen's *The Wild Duck,* whose significance is apparent only from the context of the work itself.

Language that employs symbols is clearly symbolical, but language that is spoken by a symbolic figure, whether or not it includes specific symbols, also becomes symbolical, by implication; that is, one seeks for general significance beyond the particular context of the words. The thought is raised to a symbolic level. Jesus' phrase "Turn the other cheek," although it might be interpreted literally, represents, more importantly, a symbolic act expressive of passive resistance. Thus, the use of the phrase is ordinarily symbolical in implication.

In a similar way, literary characters who are drawn larger than life or who are clearly set forth as symbolic figures may often speak lines that hold significance beyond their simplest level of meaning. One senses this quality in lines like the Ancient Mariner's cry of despair when his boat is becalmed on the sea:

> Water, water, everywhere
> Nor any drop to drink.

The context does not demand a symbolical reading, but invites it.

A symbol is also capable of compressing the emotional impact of an overwhelming experience into a brief descriptive passage.

In Book IX of *Paradise Lost,* after Eve tells Adam that she has eaten of the forbidden fruit—the act that first marks man's fall from divine grace—Milton expresses Adam's stunned sensation by two simple lines:

From his slack hand the Garland wreath'd for Eve
Down dropp'd, and all the faded Roses shed.

Symbolic language of this kind has a vividness and force far beyond any kind of ordinary description.

Imagery

Images are the mental impressions created by words in such a way that we can perceive sensations without actually experiencing them. Metaphor and symbol are, of course, common sources of imagery, but other uses of words can evoke the same kind of image-making. Imagery adds sensuousness to language. The opening quatrain of an Emily Dickinson poem is tense with sensations:

I heard a Fly buzz—when I died—
The Stillness in the Room
Was like the Stillness in the Air—
Between the Heaves of Storm—

This is not a simple contrast of sound and stillness, because worked within the images of the sound of the fly and the stillness of the room are also images of the stillness of air and the sounds of the storm like the troubled breathing of a person.

A passage from James Joyce's *Araby* also represents a complex interweaving of sense images of all varieties to create a vivid description of a winter's evening:

When the short days of winter came dusk fell before we had well eaten our dinners. When we met in the street the houses had grown sombre. The space of sky above us was the colour of ever-changing violet and towards it the lamps of the street lifted their feeble lanterns. The cold air stung us and we played till our bodies glowed. Our shouts echoed in the silent street. The career of our play brought us through the dark muddy lanes behind the houses where we ran the gauntlet of the rough tribes from the cottages, to the back doors of the dark dripping gardens where odours arose from the ashpits, to the dark odorous stables where a coachman smoothed and combed the horse or shook music from the buckled harness.

One needs only to reflect upon those details that appeal to sight, touch, hearing, and smell to perceive the rich, sensuous quality of this prose.

Besides the animated effect that imagery gives to poetry and prose, it also provides a basis for analysis. Imagery serves as an index to the author's conception of his work. In fact, if it is used with consistency, it may even mirror his interests, his experiences, and his temperament. Some writers draw constantly upon images of nature or love or domestic images or religious images; in a particular work, images may be prevailingly violent or beautiful or gloomy, images may express sadness or buoyancy or sterility. It is often possible to trace threads of imagery running throughout a work—a color scheme, a concern for sounds, an interest in animals, a sexual motif—patterns of images emerging from the writing as a means of setting the tone, of commenting on a character's actions, or indicating the author's attitude toward his material. The choice of imagery may be a clue to where the author's sympathies lie.

Not all references to color, sound, animal life, and sex are, of course, necessarily image-making. These can be discussed in quite abstract, unemotional, encyclopedic terms. But the simplest alteration can change the effect. Even a simple proverb can be expressed by fact or fancy. One proverb may attempt to explain:

> A wise man will hear, and will increase learning; and a man of understanding shall attain unto wise counsels.

Another may attempt to express its meaning by images:

> A whip for the horse, a bridle for the ass, and a rod for the fool's back.

The difference between the two is that the words in the second proverb move the imagination to perceive first, then to interpret; in the first, one need only interpret. Imagery is the link between the imagination of the writer and the imagination of the reader.

Stylized Language

What is convenient to keep in mind for purposes of analyzing language in literature is that even the most realistic work does not record speech as we ordinarily use it. The tone may seem colloquial and natural, but the dialogue we read is a conventionalized speech for literary purposes. It is highly compressed; many of the filler words are omitted. Missing also are the bland phrases that have meaning only because we speak them with a particular intonation, and absent too are the repetition and stammering that are characteristic of speech. The degree to which dialogue departs from the customary diction and rhythms of speech is the degree of its stylization. Some dialogue departs so very little from the expected patterns that we take no notice of it. It creates an illusion of conversation. On the other hand, some plays are entirely written in verse, so that the dialogue in its effect becomes stylized.

Stylization is relative and dependent to a great extent on conventions that prevail at any one particular time. Elements of an Elizabethan play that may seem highly stylized to us in the twentieth century may have seemed far less so to a sixteenth-century audience accustomed to the diction of the plays and the prevalence of verse drama at that time. In a similar way, the diction and arrangement of words of pre-twentieth-century poetry often seem highly stylized to modern ears accustomed to the words and rhythms of standard colloquial speech in the drama and poetry of today. Reading experience helps to distinguish what is customary for any particular age and what is a departure from the ordinary for special effects.

When T. S. Eliot wrote *Murder in the Cathedral* for the Canterbury Festival of 1935, he chose verse as an appropriate vehicle for the twelfth-century story of Thomas Becket. The chorus, itself a stylized device of drama, speaks in this manner:

Here is no continuing city, here is no abiding stay.
Ill the wind, ill the time, uncertain the profit, certain the danger.
O late late late, late is the time, late too late, and rotten the year;
Evil the wind, and bitter the sea, and grey the sky, grey, grey, grey.

And the Archbishop achieves high drama even in ordering the door of the cathedral to be opened:

Unbar the doors! throw open the doors!
I will not have the house of prayer, the church of Christ,
The sanctuary, turned into a fortress.
The Church shall protect her own, in her own way, not
As oak and stone; stone and oak decay,
Give no stay, but the Church shall endure.
The church shall be open, even to our enemies. Open the door!

In an essay entitled "Poetry and Drama," T. S. Eliot explains that he intended this style to be "neutral" in terms of time. It is neither twelfth-century nor modern; neither Shakespearean nor nineteenth-century. In brief, we can now look upon it as highly stylized speech that is appropriate both to the tense dramatic action, the elevated nature of the characters, and a subject drawn from the past.

Stylization may, of course, take other forms. In a German play dating from 1919, Ernst Toller's *Man and the Masses*, the characters speak in a telegraphic style. The lines are frequently short elliptical phrases like the messages of a telegram:

THE WOMAN   You! Who sent you?
THE NAMELESS ONE   The masses.
THE WOMAN   They've not forgotten me?

                        The message . . . the message . . .
THE NAMELESS ONE   My mission here is to set you free.
THE WOMAN   Freedom!
                        Life!
                        We escape? Is everything prepared?
THE NAMELESS ONE   Two keepers have been bribed.
                        There's one more at the gate. I'll strike him down.
THE WOMAN   You'd murder him . . . for me?
THE NAMELESS ONE   For the cause.
THE WOMAN   I have no right.
                        To win life through a keeper's death.
THE NAMELESS ONE   The masses have a right to you.
THE WOMAN   And the rights of the keeper?
                        Keepers are men.
THE NAMELESS ONE   We have no "men" as yet.
                        On one side, the group belonging to the mass.
                        On the other, the class belonging to the State.
THE WOMAN   Man is naked.
THE NAMELESS ONE   Mass is godlike.
THE WOMAN   Mass is not godlike.
                        Force made the mass.
                        Evils of property made the mass.
                        Mass is the movement of distress,
                        Is meek devotion . . .
                        Is terrible vengeance . . .
                        Is blinded slavery . . .
                        Is holy purpose . . .
                        Mass is a fertile field that has been trampled;
                        Mass is the choked-up, inarticulate people.
                                        (trans. by Louis Untermeyer)

The stylization is Toller's way of trying to write a completely
abstract and colorless dialogue which will communicate the intellectual substance and nothing else. The emotion arises out of the
circumstances.

In a contemporary play like Ionesco's *The Bald Soprano*, stylization takes yet another form. In this play, the characters speak
with deliberate absurdity to express the lack of communication
between people and the triviality of their concerns when they do
speak. The following lines are only a brief excerpt from a secne
between a husband and his wife as they sit facing each other:

MR. MARTIN (*musing*)   How curious it is, how curious it is, how
curious it is, and what a coincidence! You know, in my bedroom there
is a bed, and it is covered with a green eiderdown. This room, with
the bed and the green eiderdown, is at the end of the corridor between
the w.c. and the bookcase, dear lady!

MRS. MARTIN   What a coincidence, good Lord, what a coincidence!

My bedroom, too, has a green eiderdown and is at the end of the corridor, between the w.c., dear sir, and the bookcase!

MR. MARTIN   How bizarre, curious, strange! Then, madam, we live in the same room and we sleep in the same bed, dear lady. It is perhaps there that we have met!

MRS. MARTIN   How curious it is and what a coincidence! It is indeed possible that we have met there, and perhaps even last night. But I do not recall it, dear sir!

MR. MARTIN   I have a little girl, my little daughter, she lives with me, dear lady. She is two years old, she's blonde, she has a white eye and a red eye, she is very pretty, her name is Alice, dear lady.

MRS. MARTIN   What a bizarre coincidence! I, too, have a little girl. She is two years old, has a white eye and a red eye, she is very pretty, and her name is Alice, too, dear sir!

MR. MARTIN   (*in the same drawling, monotonous voice*)   How curious it is and what a coincidence! And bizarre! Perhaps they are the same, dear lady!

MRS. MARTIN   How curious it is! It is indeed possible, dear sir. (*A rather long moment of silence. The clock strikes 29 times.*)

Stylization, therefore, represents a deliberate distortion of language for a particular effect.

Paradox, Dramatic Irony, and Verbal Irony

Paradox and verbal irony work essentially on a common principle of apparent contradiction and, therefore, often arise from the same context. Paradox treats opposites in such a way that both elements of the contradiction seem to be true but in different contexts. Because a statement of this kind works contrary to what we ordinarily expect, the effect is also ironic. Irony is based on a sense of some difference: things are not as they seem; they do not turn out as they should; or there is a discrepancy between intention and effect. The irony of drama and fiction frequently depends on a situation, hence the term "dramatic irony." But irony may also be a figure of speech; hence the term "verbal irony," in which the meaning of the words is simply reversed by the ironic tone. Popular phrases like "the home of the brave," "the land of the free," or "America the beautiful" can easily be twisted to mean just their opposite.

Dramatic irony and verbal irony are at times not completely separable. Complex circumstances which are themselves paradoxical and ironic often produce language of a similar variety. Sophocles' *Oedipus the King* has become almost the standard example of the way in which dramatic irony works. The play itself is based on a series of paradoxical situations:

Oedipus the king, the savior of Thebes, is also its destroyer.
The curse he places on the killer of Laios he places on himself.
The tracker of the criminal is the criminal himself.
Teiresias, who is blind, can see; Oedipus, who can see, is blind.

Each element of these paradoxes holds true because Oedipus, the savior and king of Thebes, is also without his own knowledge the slayer of his father Laios. Separated from his father as a child, he later unknowingly kills him. Thus, the lines of the play are constant sources of irony and paradox. When Oedipus prays that the guilty man waste his life away, he concludes his speech with highly ironic words:

> In my house, I knowing it, he dwells,
> May every curse I spake on my head fall.

Without knowing it, he is the one in his own house on whom the curse has fallen.

A later speech turns on the paradox of seeing and not seeing. After the blind Teiresias has told Oedipus that he is the murderer of his father and the scourge of the land, Oedipus speaks:

> In one long night thou liv'st, and can'st not hurt,
> Or me, or any man who sees the light.

Oedipus' mocking of Teiresias as one who cannot hurt him because he cannot see produces irony because all that Teiresias speaks is true and will bring about Oedipus' grief and tragedy.

Irony, however, does not always strike a serious note. The unexpected turn of events that Marvell describes in a short couplet from "To His Coy Mistress" produces a touch of ironic humor:

> The Grave's a fine and private place,
> But none I think do there embrace.

Likewise, the paradox may be comic as well as serious. A short poem by John Donne gives this effect:

> *Antiquary*
> If in his study he hath so much care
> To hang all old, strange things, let his wife beware.

Irony and paradox can be sought out in almost any literary work, because their concern with self-contradiction is implicit in almost all experience, if one will choose to see it. They can easily be missed unless one reads with an eye and ear for them. They demand that the reader be able to think from more than one point of view. They ask him to flip a coin to see what is on the other side. They demonstrate that the literary artist typically does not see everyday life with a single and simple aim. If he does so, he risks superficiality or dogmatism. Paradox and irony are both literary ways of coping with many of the seemingly unresolvable complexities of experience. As expression, they do not offer solutions. They merely reflect the nature of things to help us understand.

Ambiguity and Punning

Ambiguity and punning, like irony and paradox, turn upon double meanings. Words are used so that they have more than one implication. Punning is basically a twist of a familiar expression ("There's method in his gladness"); a play upon words that are spelled differently but sound alike (Max Beerbohm, asked to hike to the top of a Swiss mountain, declined by saying, "I am an anti-climb Max"); a play upon a single word that may have several possible meanings (*Hamlet:* 'T is for the dead, not for the quick, therefore thou liest. *First Clown:* 'T is a quick lie, sir; 't will away again, from me to you.).

Punning is most commonly written for a comic effect, but when the situation is a serious one the effect is gently ironic. The literature of the past indicates that writers did not consider it amiss to pun in serious situations. Dylan Thomas seems to follow that tradition in these lines from "Do Not Go Gentle into That Good Night":

Grave men, near death, who see with blinding sight
Blind eyes could blaze like meteors and be gay,
Rage, rage against the dying of the light.

The opening line is reminiscent of the speech of the dying Mercutio in *Romeo and Juliet:*

. . . ask for me tomorrow, and you shall find me a grave man.

Ambiguity, however, has broader possibilities than punning alone. Generally to be avoided in expository prose because of the uncertainty of meaning that arises, it is intentionally used in literature as a way of revealing the paradoxes and ironies of life which plague thoughtful men. In this sense, ambiguity adds richness of suggestion to the language.

In particular scenes of *Hamlet,* the ambiguity of Hamlet's remarks is appropriate to the character, for one can never be wholly certain when the frenzy of his emotions has carried his feigned madness into true madness. One such scene is his conversation with Ophelia, which follows immediately his thoughts of suicide in the soliloquy "To be or not to be." He taunts Ophelia with questions that are deliberately ambiguous, that seem to doubt her chastity but on the surface could mean something else:

HAMLET Ha, ha! Are you honest?

OPHELIA My lord?
HAMLET Are you fair?
OPHELIA What means your lordship?

The ambiguity carries over into his phrase "Get thee to a nunnery. Why would'st thou be a breeder of sinners?" A nunnery is a
place of refuge from the world, but Elizabethan audiences would
also have known the word as a cant term for a bawdy house.
The ambiguity in these lines suggests Hamlet's divided thinking
and complicated state of mind, both his concern for Ophelia in this
scene and his bitterness toward her.

Ambiguity frequently results when feelings are mixed. At
times, the writer may not convey with certainty and clarity what
he feels or thinks. In a short poem, "Dust of Snow," Robert
Frost leaves his "change of mood" unexplained:

> The way a crow
> Shook down on me
> The dust of snow
> From a hemlock tree
>
> Has given my heart
> A change of mood
> And saved some part
> Of a day I had rued.

It is clear that the falling snow has changed his spirits for the
good, but the precise nature of his new mood remains ambiguous.
What realization has the experience brought about? Should one
place emphasis upon *the way* the crow shook down the dust of
snow? In this instance, the vagueness of situation and feeling
makes the miniature poem a source of wonder and suggestiveness.
Ambiguity, like many other effects of language, demands of a
reader the kind of imaginative participation that ultimately draws
him into the experience so that he must weigh what he, as well as
the writer, understands by the language he reads.

Verbal Humor

Verbal humor is itself an ambiguous effect because it depends on
a reader's responding to an incongruity between the statement
and the writer's intention. If the incongruity is lost on the reader,
the effect is lost. Some people do not see humor where others do.

Incongruity can exist only in terms of some norm. If incongruity means that something is out of keeping, it is logical to ask
in terms of what. Verbal humor has direct reference to ordinary
communicable speech, which maintains a semblance of rea-
sonable tone, uniform usage, and orderliness. Any departures from
these general norms are capable of producing something comical.

Verbal humor has three main sources: disproportion, surprise, and confusion.

Disproportion is the incongruity that arises between the way something is said and what has actually happened. It is therefore the stock and trade of the braggart, the bluffer, and the teller of tall tales. Falstaff's speeches are funny because he is all three of these. In *Henry IV, Part 1,* in the scene at the Boar's Head Tavern in Eastcheap, Falstaff makes a fool of himself by boasting how he overcame a dozen rogues on the road near Gadshill:

> I am a rogue if I were not at half-sword with a dozen of them two hours together. I have 'scaped by miracle. I am eight times thrust through the doublet, four through the hose; my buckler cut through and through; my sword hacked like a handsaw—*ecce signum!* I never dealt better since I was a man. All would not do. A plague of all cowards! Let them speak. If they speak more or less than truth, they are villains and the sons of darkness.

Falstaff speaks more than truth, because from an earlier scene the audience knows that Falstaff and his three companions were set upon as a prank by Poins and Prince Hal and that, when attacked, all of them ran, leaving behind them the money they themselves had robbed from pilgrims on the road. As Falstaff is later prodded into telling the incident, the numbers grow from 12 to 16 to 22 or 23 and finally to the climactic figure:

> If there were not two or three and fifty upon old Jack, than am I no two-legged creature.

Falstaff's story is amusing, not only in the exaggeration with which he tells it but in the way he draws it out. It is disproportionate in its hyperbole and its length.

The second source of verbal humor, surprise, is the incongruity that arises between what is said and what is expected to be said. This kind of humor almost always shifts the tone the author has established, so that a sudden contrast produces a comic effect. One amusing scene in Bernard Shaw's *Pygmalion* is when Eliza Doolittle, who has been taught to speak the King's English with propriety, shocks a small group of socialites by letting a vulgarism slip into her speech. Asked by Freddy if she is going to walk across the park, she responds: "Walk! Not bloody likely. I am going in a taxi." The humor is often lost on American audiences because they fail to respond in the same way that proper Englishmen would to the word "bloody." In the musical *My Fair Lady,* based on this play, the device is repeated, but the scene is shifted to a race track and a phrase used that American audiences would immediately recognize as an outrageous breech of language etiquette. Saying the unexpected is a common source of humor and one that Shaw commonly used in his writing.

A third source of verbal humor is confusion. It is the incongruity between the disorderliness of what is said and the coherence of what is expected. It is the humor of nonsense. Since the device is more common in spoken than written humor, it is more likely to be found in drama. The fools in Shakespeare's plays are often given confusing word-play and absurd non-sequiturs. In *Twelfth Night* (III, i), a short dialogue occurs between Viola, disguised as a young man, and a clown, carrying his tabor, a small drum:

> VIOLA   Save thee, friend, and thy music! Dost thou live by thy tabor?
> CLOWN   No, sir, I live by the church.
> VIOLA   Art thou a churchman?
> CLOWN   No such matter, sir. I do live by the church; for I do live at my house, and my house doth stand by the church.
> VIOLA   So thou mayst say, the king lies by a beggar, if a beggar dwell near him; or, the church stands by thy tabor, if thy tabor stand by the church.

This is a way, as the Clown himself says, of showing "how quickly the wrong side may be turned outward."

In Eugene Ionesco's farce *The Lesson,* the Professor tutoring his young pupil walks up and down the room as he delivers a nonsensical lecture on the neo-Spanish languages:

> That which distinguishes the neo-Spanish languages from each other and their idioms from the other linguistic groups, such as the group of languages called Austrian and neo-Austrian or Hapsburgian, as well as the Esperanto, Helvetian, Monacan, Swiss, Andorran, Basque, and jai alai groups, and also the groups of diplomatic and technical languages—that which distinguishes them, I repeat, is their striking resemblance which makes it so hard to distinguish them from each other—I'm speaking of the neo-Spanish languages which one is able to distinguish from each other, however, only thanks to their distinctive characteristics, absolutely indisputable proofs of their extraordinary resemblance, which renders indisputable their common origin, and which, at the same time, differentiates them profoundly—through the continuation of the distinctive traits which I've just cited.

Variations of this kind of humor occur in any repartee in which wordplay predominates.

Satire

When humor is given a target, it becomes satire. Satire mixes humor with criticism. Yet not all satire balances the elements of humor and criticism equally. Two traditions have continued since Roman times: one of satire written with geniality and urbanity in the manner of Horace; one of anger and violent lashing out against evil in the manner of Juvenal. The proportion of humor or criticism produces literary works of a quite different nature. If the element of criticism is lost altogether, the work becomes empty farce. If the humor is lost altogether, the work degenerates into invective. Ideally, satire may be said to lie somewhere between the extremes of buffoonery and verbal abuse. Yet since satirists are not of one temperament, the English language offers a generous supply of words to suggest various tones and forms of satire: derision, invective, vituperation, jeremiad, raillery, ridicule, mockery, *reductio ad absurdum*, sarcasm, irony, caricature, parody, burlesque, comedy of manners, mock-epic, *commedia dell' arte*, clownishness, farce. In each of these, satire exists to a greater or lesser degree; the scale ranges from bitter scorn to gentle irony to sidesplitting laughter.

Since satire is actually a mode of perception—a predisposition —which shapes the writer's thought and language, it needs to be discussed in terms of a work as a whole. Unless the reader catches the writer's intention at an early stage, the effect can be lost or misinterpreted. Even the grotesquerie of Swift's "A Modest Proposal" was read straight by members of the eighteenth-century audience, and in our own time some readers fail to perceive the satire of some of their favorite nursery rhymes.

The twist the satiric manner represents may be illustrated by the first stanzas of a series of poems that use Marlowe's "The Passionate Shepherd to His Love" as a point of departure. Marlowe's poem is an effervescent expression of love in an idyllic scene:

Come live with me and be my love,
And we will all the pleasures prove,
That valleys, groves, hills and fields,
And all the craggy mountains yields.

In response, Sir Walter Ralegh wrote "The Nymph's Reply to the Shepherd":

If all the world and love were young
And truth in every shepherd's tongue,
These pretty pleasures might me move,
To live with thee, and be thy love.

Here the note of skepticism in the opening lines gives the poem a gentle satiric edge.

Some thirty or more years later, John Donne wrote another version entitled "The Bait":

Come live with me and be my love,
And we will some new pleasures prove,
Of golden sands, and crystal brooks,
With silken lines, and silver hooks.

Donne's switch of the scene throughout his poem from valleys and mountains to sands and streams to pursue a metaphor of his love swimming in the river as bait for "enamoured fish" adds a touch of absurdity that makes the poem virtually a parody of the delicate sentiments of Marlowe's poem.

Yet another poem, this one of the twentieth century, C. Day Lewis' "Come, Live With Me and Be My Love," adds the strongest hint of satire by again imitating the poem that extols pastoral delights that are no more:

Come, live with me and be my love,
And we will all the pleasures prove
Of peace and plenty, bed and board,
That chance employment may afford.

These are examples of genial satire, a mockery of Marlowe's starry-eyed but charming view of young love.

In hard-hitting satire, the laugh fades quickly or the pleasantry takes the shape of a sardonic grin. E. E. Cummings, however, is one of the contemporary writers who maintained a firm grip on humor even when he was being most devastating in his comment. His poem "my sweet old etcetera" represents the art of satire at its best; the criticism and the humor come through equally clear:

my sweet old etcetera
aunt lucy during the recent
war could and what
is more did tell you just
what everybody was fighting

for,
my sister

isabel created hundreds
(and
hundreds)of socks not to
mention shirts fleaproof earwarmers

etcetera wristers etcetera, my
mother hoped that

i would die etcetera

bravely of course my father used
to become hoarse talking about how it was
a privilege and if only he
could meanwhile my

self etcetera lay quietly
in the deep mud et

cetera
(dreaming,   '
et

   cetera, of
Your smile
eyes knees and of your Etcetera)

SUGGESTIONS FOR WRITING ABOUT LANGUAGE

Since literature is a verbal art, it is the word that makes possible all of
its effects—not the isolated word, but the word set down appropriately
with other words; the words shaped in forms that reveal the author's plan;
the words arranged with timing so that the pace and tone are varied; the
words chosen imaginatively so that the writer's intentions and feelings
are implicit in the style as well as the thought and characters and actions.
The language of a literary work can be examined as an end in itself, but
ordinarily the language is studied as a source of tone, atmosphere, pacing,
characterization, and the implied thoughts of the writer as well as his
explicit statements.

Questions like the following therefore suggest possible leads for the
discussion of language in literature:

1. Is the language appropriate to the narrator? Does his dialect and style
   differentiate him from the author?
2. Is the speech of characters in the work differentiated? Does a major
   part of the characterization spring from the way a character speaks,
   as opposed to the way he acts? To what extent does the dialogue
   create an illusion of reality? To what extent is it conventionalized?
   Does the author depend on certain techniques for recording speech?
3. Is the language stylized? To what degree? For what purpose? Does
   stylization seem to draw attention away from the matter of the work
   to the manner?
4. Are images and symbols natural or contrived? Universal or occasional? To what extent do they seem forcibly imposed on the material? What is gained by images that hit on extremely unlikely comparisons? In what way is the imagery an index to the writer's
   personality and mind? In what way can the metaphors be paraphrased
   so that the full meaning emerges?

5. What are the consistent mental and emotional impressions that emerge from reading the work? What areas of experience are drawn from? Do these follow a pattern? Do the sources and patterns comment on the characters? On the author? Do they create a special tone or atmosphere?

6. What explanations can be given that will resolve a paradox? What relation does paradoxical language have to the action and the characters? What relation does paradox have to the author's state of mind?

7. What different meanings grow out of a particular example of verbal ambiguity? What are the implications of any one of them? From what source does ambiguity arise? From the words? From the syntax? From general vagueness? From the tone? Does the thought and structure of the work as a whole help to settle on one interpretation in preference to another?

8. In what terms can the author's language be characterized? Highly figurative or symbolical? Abstract? Colloquial? Mixed? What is the general appropriateness of the language to the theme of the work?

9. What is the source of verbal humor? What is its purpose? Is it used for contrast, diversion, satire? If it is satiric, what is being mocked?

10. What manner does the writer assume to satirize? Is anger evident, moral indignation, geniality, fun? How do these qualities promote criticism?

7
Stylistic Effects

Strategies and Nonverbal Effects

Literary style can refer to a number of different things: the style of a writer, the style of a particular work, the style of a period. These obviously are not independent of one another: writers produce the works that establish the characteristic manner of a movement. Yet the range of emphasis between the writer and the period is great enough to cause confusion about what style actually is. Where does it exist? In the writer? In the product? In the mind of the reader?

In this discussion, "style" will be used as a term to refer to the effect which grows out of a writer's ways of working with elements that combine to make up a literary work. Style can be discussed in terms of any one of the components: the arrangement of the plot, the details of the setting, the manner of characterization, the effects of form, the choice and arrangement of language, the modes of thought and feeling. In these terms, almost all writing about literature is in some way a discussion of style. Yet beyond particular focuses of this kind, style can also be discussed as a cumulative effect of the various strategies used, as a total impression gained by the reader as he reads and reacts. Style is therefore not infrequently discussed in highly impressionistic and metaphorical terms. While he was studying the style of Jonathan Swift, Professor Louis Milic collected a group of adjectives used by critics to describe the writing of Swift. His partial list includes words like *charming, clear, common, concise, correct, direct, elaborate, elegant, energetic, graceful, hard-round-crystalline, homely, lucid, manly, masculine, muscular, nervous, ornamented, perfect, plain, poor, proper, pure, salty, simple, sinewy, sonorous,* and *vigorous.* Some of these are so different that one wonders if the critics had read the same writer. Of course, writers do not always maintain a consistent and invariable style, so that generalizations may legitimately vary. Writers experiment; they come under new influences; they change with age. Even though we think of their minds and personalities as relatively constant, they may change in philosophy and temperament with age.

Meaningful discussions of style, therefore, are those that are most specific while at the same time attempting to explain what effects grow out of the writing. The effect of style cannot be dismissed as an illusion, because even after all of the strategies have been explained, the structures analyzed, and the words diagnosed, the dimensions of style extend further into areas of sensory and extrasensory perception. These effects are often contextual; they can be explained only in terms of the whole, as the effect of the parts interacting together. In these terms, a number of stylistic features contribute to the readability of literature.

Climax and Suspense

Climax is a part of the dynamics of a literary work. It is a point of culmination, a moment of high tension and involvement. Thus a work might possibly have a number of climactic incidents, but the main one is usually apparent—the confrontation, the discovery, the revelation, the realization, the final struggle—whatever may be the high point of interest on which the story turns. Tracing the action to a point of climax is a way of recognizing how the writer has built his story and involved the reader in the process.

Suspense is a tension caused by looking forward. It is the anticipation that accumulates before the climax is reached and is generally limited to works that withhold crucial information from the reader. If the entire story is known to the reader in advance, suspense is minimized. Both Greek and modern works based on familiar myths have little suspense because the outcome of the events is known from the beginning. The primary interest lies in the writer's way of working out the narrative and his interpretation of the characters and actions. The interest in such works is, therefore, focused on different aspects of style.

Works in which the outcome of the action is unknown generate a strong element of suspense. Thus, the courtroom and trial by jury are a natural setting and situation for suspense. Detective fiction and adventure stories depend heavily on suspense as a main source of interest.

Pace

All writing is based on motion. It is not a static art, as the words on the printed page might lead one to believe. We not uncommonly speak of the pace of a work. Pace is a matter of timing, both the writer's own sense of movement in developing his ideas and the reader's sense of how the writing moves. A slow pace encourages reflection; it also risks boredom. A rapid pace magnetizes the reader; it also risks superficiality. Long works, therefore, are paced so that the movement is sometimes slowed, sometimes quickened. The novelist's sense of timing may not be unlike the strategy of a long-distance runner; he cannot go the whole distance at the same speed.

Pace is often a matter of the relation between action, description, and dialogue, but it is also a matter of specific technique. In poetry, for example, the metrical line has the effect of moving the verse more quickly or slowly. A regular line which runs smoothly and uninterruptedly tends to move quickly. A metrical variation usually tends to slow the rhythm. In a long work like *Paradise Lost,* consisting of more than 10,000 lines of blank verse, Milton depends on deviations from the regular line to vary the effects. In two succeeding lines (108–109) from Book IV, the pace changes noticeably:

> So farewell hope, and, with hope, farewell fear,
> Farewell remorse! All good to me is lost;

In the second regular line, the pace quickens.

Frequently, the pace of a line suits the thought. The description of Satan's journey through the realms of Chaos and Night (II, 949–950) reflects his changing progress, sometimes fast, sometimes slow:

> So eagerly the Fiend
> O'er bog or steep, through strait, rough, dense, or rare,
> With head, hands, wings, or feet, pursues his way,
> And swims, or sinks, or wades, or creeps, or flies.

In another description of motion (II, 618–621), the final line of eight stressed syllables reflects the arduous progress against obstacles:

> Through many a dark and dreary vale
> They passed, and many a region dolorous,
> O'er many a frozen, many a fiery alp,
> Rocks, caves, lakes, fens, bogs, dens, and shades of death.

These, of course, are variations only within the pattern of blank verse. They do not take into account the variety of pace that can be achieved by different metrical patterns, short and long lines, and the variations within those patterns. Versification is the poet's special way of controlling the pace of his words.

The prose style of fiction can also strongly affect the pace of a work. There is little doubt that the characteristic sentence patterns of Melville, James, or Faulkner cause their prose to move at a slower pace than that of Lawrence, Hemingway, or Sherwood Anderson. But, in general, the pace of fiction is much more a matter of the rate at which the narrative moves forward. The action can move ahead rapidly in a linear sense or hesitate and move in a vertical direction, so that the writer or his characters in a sense stop the action to probe, reflect, or philosophize. In long works, there are alternate horizontal and vertical movements. A story of little action in which most of the movement is vertical may well be highly static, not dull as a consequence, but interesting in terms of other than straight storytelling.

The narrative technique of a story may also affect its pace. A cinematic technique, basically one in which fragments are projected before the reader without obvious transitions between them, is designed as a kind of economical narration. It is less concerned with the linear quality of narration and more with the total effect. It operates like a collage. On the other hand, a story in which the transitions are carefully drawn so that all of the parts are linked and interfused to make a continuous whole may move with less obvious sense of speed, but the logic of its narration may make it read more easily so that it seems to move at an equally rapid pace. Pace is a matter of intuitive perception in fiction, not unrelated to the technique the writer is using.

In drama, pace is largely a matter of the relation between action and dialogue. The drama is not a form that invites large-scale action. If the background is war, the action ordinarily takes place offstage or between acts. The clashes of rival forces onstage in some of Shakespeare's history plays inevitably fail to convey a sense of intense conflict because stage drama is primarily a form for talking about action, not showing it. When a story or play is converted to film, however, more action is always included simply because cinema, with its greater flexibility and pace, is capable of showing far more. To go to the other extreme, when there is almost no action at all in a stage play and only talk remains, then the movement must depend entirely on the pace of the talk—the dialogue.

One notable development in twentieth-century drama has been writers' interest in discursive plays—plays in which the characters drawn together in a common crisis simply talk. Nothing of significance happens; the reader's interest must be in the characters as speakers, or there is no interest. Many of Shaw's plays, particularly one like *St. Joan,* fall into this category. Plays by Giraudoux, Beckett, and Ionesco are similarly discursive. Plays of this kind differ from others in that they lack a strong narrative base. All drama is composed of speaking, and in none is language more important than in Greek tragedies, which traditionally relegated violent action to offstage. Yet these plays were not without violent action. The tragedies were tragedies of dying, not the modern tragedies of living and talking about it. The pace of drama, therefore, seems to relate primarily to the kinds of things characters talk about and the length at which they expound. Drama that utilizes the natural pace of conversation with a strong sense of a developing action is likely to move at a far brisker pace than one in which characters make speeches and only wait for their fate.

Tone and Atmosphere

The tone of a literary work derives primarily from the choices and combinations of words that writers use, and we identify these stylistic effects as irony, satire, humor, understatement, hyperbole, or ambiguity. These verbal qualities have already been discussed in the previous section, "Language, Symbol, and Imagery." Tone, however, may also result from the reader's response to form and rhetorical design, like orderliness or balance. What impresses us as a tone of eloquence in a work may be largely a result of emphasis or repetition or parallelism. Or what impresses us as unpleasant may be a writer's deliberate attempt to avoid the euphony of liquid sounds, appealing alliterations, or rhymes. All of these are tone qualities with which every writer has to be concerned if he is at all interested in more than the simple act of communication. In literature, tone is more than the tone of the language. It also depends on other effects which are essentially nonverbal in nature. These can be grouped as typographical and theatrical.

Typographical Effects

Typographical effects include both the use of various kinds of type styles for dramatic effect and the arrangement of words on a page for a rhetorical effect. Both devices are deliberate attempts to escape the most routine form of presentation on the printed page. They force a reader to respond because they deviate from customary practices. The now familiar appearance of the name of e e cummings without capital letters and punctuation reminds us of the kind of awareness we have of changes from conventional practice. Cummings' own poems are familiar examples of rearrangements of words which will not permit the reader to view them thoughtlessly. Such rearrangements are a visual attempt to get away from the routine, just as a fresh image is an attempt to escape the cliché. Or they may be an attempt to get beyond the medium of words—to suggest motion or to appeal to the visual image. Any alteration of type, mechanics, line length, form, or spacing needs to be considered for the purpose the author had in mind.

Many typographical variations, particularly in fiction, may be best characterized as nonbook effects. They imitate the more spectacular appeals of newspaper and magazine techniques or they seem to borrow from the movie script or television commercial. Even though some readers may dismiss these as cheap and superficial effects, the conclusion cannot be avoided that they are operating in their own nonverbal way to contribute to the tone of a work.

Theatrical Effects

Aristotle, one of the earliest writers on dramatic theory, recognized both music and spectacle as parts of dramatic effect, even though he spoke of them as accessories rather than as essential components. Any overemphasis on them he would have considered a distraction from a tragedy's purpose. The history of dramatic production indicates that the elaborateness of staging has varied with fashion and the availability of resources. Yet before the modern period, the resources of the stage seem to have been looked on as supplemental to the writer's script—something added to give the play dramatic life on the stage. The play could be seen with the additions, but it could also with equal force be read without them. Its meaning was in the language, not in the acting, the lights, and the sounds.

Many modern dramatists, however, have experimented with theatrical resources in an effect to establish tone and atmosphere as a new dimension of meaning. Thus a language of pantomime, light, and sound at times substitutes for the language of words. The result is that meaning becomes more and more implicit rather than explicit, expressive rather than reasoned, sensuous rather than discursive. These are plays written to be experienced; reading them requires a special kind of imaginative interpretation.

The final stage direction of Ionesco's *Exit the King* is a good example:

Sudden disappearance of QUEEN MARGUERITE *on the left. The* KING *is seated on his throne. During this final scene, the doors, windows and walls of the throne room will have slowly disappeared. This part of the action is very important.*

Now there is nothing on the stage except the KING *on his throne in a grayish light. Then the* KING *and his throne also disappear.*

Finally, there is nothing but the gray light.

This disappearance of the windows, the doors and the walls, the KING *and the throne must be very marked, but happen slowly and gradually. The* KING *sitting on his throne should remain visible for a short time before fading into a kind of mist.*

This particular ending is a tableau in which the most important commentary is made by the language of silence and light. The fade-out is more than a representation of lights going off or night coming on; it is a vehicle that depicts emotionally and symbolically the experience of death and man's disappearance into the unknown darkness.

Many effects of lighting and sound and mime that the dramatist writes into his directions are not intended to create an illusion. In fact, they may work directly to the contrary. They make the audience aware that the theater is a theater; that characters are actors playing roles; that real life is not being enacted on the stage. At the end of Edward Albee's *The American Dream,* Grandma interrupts the dialogue to speak directly to the audience:

GRANDMA *(interrupting . . . to audience)*   Well, I guess that just about wraps it up. I mean, for better or worse, this is a comedy, and I don't think we'd better go any further. No, definitely not. So, let's leave things as they are right now . . . while everybody's happy . . . while everybody's got what he wants . . . or everybody's got what he thinks he wants. Good night, dears.

In its effect, the speech functions somewhat like the ancient Greek chorus, which remained on stage as an observer and commented on the action.

The stage has definite limitations, but the nonverbal effects are definite attempts to transcend the limitations and to use them to advantage. At the beginning of Tennessee Williams' *The Glass Menagerie*, Tom, the narrator and also a character in the play, addresses the audience. After speaking of the social background of the play, he says:

> The play is memory. Being a memory play, it is dimly lighted, it is sentimental, it is not realistic. In memory everything seems to happen to music. That explains the fiddle in the wings.

These few remarks indicate the extent to which the music and the lighting are an integral part of this play. They must be taken into account not only for production purposes but for reading purposes as well.

In this same play, Williams planned to use a slide projector which would cast titles and images on one of the walls of the stage. The device was not actually used in the original Broadway production, but is written into the published manuscript. Williams explains the use of the slides as a structural device—as a means of giving a narrative line to an episodic play, and as a way of accenting values in particular scenes. Some of the legends read, "After the fiasco," "You think I'm in love with continental shoemakers?" "Things have a way of turning out so badly." The images include "Amanda as a girl on a porch, greeting callers," "Sailing vessel with jolly roger," "Blue Roses," and a "Glamor magazine cover." The screen images, therefore, serve additional purposes: they act as a memory device, they comment on the action, and they create atmosphere.

Theatrical effects of this kind cannot be ignored in reading a play. In fact, stage directions from the time of Ibsen on become increasingly important as explanations of the writer's intentions. They are not exit-and-entrance instructions; they are interpretations. A reader and interpreter of drama, particularly of modern drama, must therefore assume the mental role of director, scenic designer, and choreographer in an effort to determine fully the implications of the dramatist's directions. In this way, he must try to interpret the way nonverbal effects have been made an essential part of the style of the work.

SUGGESTIONS FOR WRITING ABOUT STYLISTIC EFFECTS

In order to avoid the pitfall of writing only vague generalizations about style, a reader needs to focus his attention on specific strategies that the writer is using to create his effects. The reader's impressions and emotional responses are by no means to be ignored, although they should be only the starting point. The reader has to ask himself why he responds as he does. Why is he interested? Why must he read to the end without stopping? Why is he moved to pause and reflect? What makes the style compelling?

To get at particular strategies that often make a writer's style what it is, questions like the following provide leads for the discussion of style in understandable and concrete terms:

1. What words best characterize the style of a particular work? Does this manner of style seem to predominate in other works by the same writer? Is there one style of the writer that seems to include many different manners?
2. What are identifiable strategies the writer is using? What are they accomplishing stylistically?
3. What are the climactic points in a novel or play? Do these seem to build to one main climax? Do these seem to set up a rhythmic pattern of stress and lack of stress, like the meter of a poem?
4. Where does the main climax occur in relation to the end? Is there an abrupt dénouement after the climax or a continuation of the story? What is the effect of either strategy?
5. What are the main elements that sustain the reader's interest in the literary work? What anticipations are set up? Are there other kinds of suspense than the one that depends on withheld information or wondering what will happen? Can the emotional effects of the literary work on the reader be explained in terms of suspense?
6. What elements can be identified which affect the pace of a long work? In fiction, what is the balance of action, description, and dialogue? What makes a drama static or fast moving? Is pace also related to climax and suspense?
7. In what way are the metrics of a poem suitable to its thought? What are the effects that derive almost completely from the versification? What is the degree of irregularity in the meter? Are the lines long or short or alternating?
8. What is the predominant tone of a work? Do the words that best describe the tone tend to be highly metaphorical? Can the impressions be supported by direct reference to particular incidents, scenes, and speeches?
9. What nonverbal resources does the writer utilize? What human senses are responding to these strategies? How many are being used simultaneously? To what effect?
10. Does the use of music, symbolic action, or light tend to support the general tone of the work and act in conjunction with the thought? Or do they tend to be accessories? Or do they serve as an ironic commentary on the characters and actions? What are the nonverbal effects doing? What would change if they were omitted? In what different ways could a play be produced to get different effects?

8

Thought and Meaning

The previous elements of literature we have discussed—the characters, the action, the setting, the structure, the language, and the style—all go to make up the literary vehicle. They are the elements that in special ways make a poem a poem or a story a story. The remaining element hinges on the writer's purpose. Why did he write what he did in the first place? What is he saying?

John Ciardi has written a book entitled *How Does a Poem Mean?* He explains that an alternate title might have been "How to talk about a poem without paraphrasing." The title of his book can readily be extended to the other forms: How does a novel mean? How does a short story mean? How does a play mean? The answers may begin to shape themselves if we ask, by contrast: How does an essay mean? How does a telegram mean? In every instance, the form itself is a part of the meaning because the author has deliberately chosen it as his way of expressing his meaning in preference to some other way.

From Literal to Metaphorical

Readers who are intent on finding "messages" in literature are applying the principles of the telegram to works that are not operating on those same principles. This is not to say that many poems, stories, and plays do not have explicit statements to make;

but it is to say that they do not usually make them with the directness and literalness of the expository statement. In "Song of Myself," Walt Whitman writes:

> I find letters from God dropt in the street, and every one is sign'd by God's name.

Paradoxically, this line uses the letter, a literal form of communication, as a metaphor. In the three preceding lines, Whitman says much more literally what he means:

> Why should I wish to see God better than this day?
> I see something of God each hour of the twenty-four, and each moment then,
> In the faces of men and women I see God, and in my own face in the glass.

To be quite explicit: the letters Whitman refers to are not written ones; they are implied in everything around us; they are metaphors of God. In a similar way, an author does not write letters to his readers in stories, poems, and plays; he communicates by everything he creates, sometimes by simply holding up a glass for us to see ourselves.

The Availability of Meaning

The obliqueness of the author's technique does not preclude writing about his thought, although it may be impossible to reduce everything to one generalization which accounts for the work as a whole. Occasionally, a summary can be made in terms of a thesis statement; for example, Turgenev's *Fathers and Sons* reveals the clash that occurs between the old and the young when the values of the older generation can no longer be accepted as the values of the younger. At other times, the meaning may be stated in terms of the commanding image: the thought and tone of Sartre's *No Exit* are expressed by the metaphor of its own title: life is a room with no escape; hell is other people. When the author has come to an understanding about life, when he has formed attitudes, when he has opinions and possibly even solutions to problems, his own convictions come through clearly, so that a reader can reduce the thought to a simple statement. This is not to imply that the thought is simple or superficial, only that it is clear and inferable.

All works, however, are not reducible in these terms. The author may claim to have no understanding of what he sees and knows, but by revealing his thoughts he may bring about awareness and understanding in others. Some literary works, particularly poems, are only observations; others are explorations with no discoveries; others are conjectures, grasping for balance and hope. To say precisely what the author's thought is in works of this kind may be impossible. He may have only a view. He may have an idea only in the sense that an idea is a predication of some kind, however diffuse: life is a lunatic asylum or a circus or a brothel. His sights may be set on fragmentation, dislocation, and discontent, not unity, order, and stability. Those who want answers in literature may not find them in writers who see their role primarily as recorders of experience, not as seers and teachers.

The important thing in writing about the thought of a literary work is not to begin with a single expectation: that the thought is there to be read as it is in an essay, open and available. The reader must expect to reach for the thought, not to have it handed to him. In works in which the meaning must be inferred, the thoughts are not hidden in the sense that they are removed from view or that they are deliberately secluded to make understanding difficult. Most authors write to be read and understood, but the most thoughtful ones are seldom reductionists. They do not find platitudes and clichés adequate expressions for their insights. They may find it necessary to work out the meaning of a story or a poem in complex ways. It is certainly a legitimate question to ask what a writer is driving at as long as we do not always expect to be able to come up with a quick and easy answer.

How Literature Means

To consider how a story or a poem or a play means is to go beyond what the words say. Meaning is not limited strictly to ideas, to its intellectual substance and sense. Meaning cannot always be summarized in a sentence because works of literature have other varieties of meaning. They mean by the feelings they convey; they mean by the attitudes they create; they mean by the style they assume; they mean in terms of the author's intentions and the time and occasion of his or her writing. Accordingly, new meanings emerge constantly with the passage of time and with the investigations of new readers. Thus, writing about the meaning of a work is always justified because it can never be set down definitively at one particular time. An old work in a new time may be a revelation to its readers. A new reader is capable of seeing new meanings.

Intrinsic Sources of Thought

Even though the total meaning may be a matter of putting together the parts or drawing out inferences, particular ideas can be derived from a number of different sources within the work itself. These are intrinsic sources of thought as opposed to those which are imposed on the work from without. These intrinsic sources are built into the structure itself and, like all meaning, vary from the literal to the metaphorical. Clues to thought and meaning come from four kinds of sources:

Titles

The title ought always to be taken into account; it may hold a key to the author's emphasis and tone. Ibsen's play *Hedda Gabler* is named after the protagonist. It could be a quite literal title like Flaubert's *Madame Bovary* or Tolstoy's *Anna Karenina.* *Hedda Gabler* is different, however, because in the play Hedda Gabler is married; her name has been changed to Hedda Tesman. In the title, therefore, Ibsen hints at an idea about the main character which is developed throughout the play.

Shaw's title *Arms and the Man* provides a humorous ambiguity; the play concerns both war and romance. In addition, the title is an echo of the opening lings of Vergil's *Aeneid,* another tale of war and romance, but Shaw's play is a satire. Its title therefore suggests its mock-heroic tone. On the other hand, Hemingway's title *A Farewell to Arms,* also a story of war and romance, contains the same ambiguity, but in its combination with "farewell" suggests a tone of serious irony rather than light mockery.

A standard trick question is to ask who the Merchant of Venice is in Shakespeare's play of that name. Why does the title place the emphasis on Antonio when many people think the play is about Shylock? The title invites another way of looking at the play. Joyce's *Ulysses* and Shaw's *Pygmalion* direct the reader's attention to sources outside the works as keys to their understanding. Dickens' *Bleak House,* a novel about people's entanglements with the law, and Whitman's *Drum-Taps,* his collection of poems about the Civil War, establish a tone. Jane Austen's titles *Pride and Prejudice* and *Sense and Sensibility* give the key themes for interpreting these works. Titles like Thomas Wolfe's *Look Homeward, Angel* and Faulkner's *The Sound and the Fury* are literary allusions and therefore metaphorical in their implications. O'Neill's *The Hairy Ape* and Ibsen's *Ghosts* are also metaphorical titles which provide a commanding image for the play's meaning as a whole. Titles need to be carefully examined.

Names

The names of characters and places may have special appropriateness or irony. At times, they may actually mean something significant in terms of the play, as the name Oedipus means "swollen feet." As a baby, Oedipus had been exposed to the elements with his feet pierced and bound, left to die because the oracle of Apollo had told Laios, his father, that he would die by the hands of his own son. Or the names may invite an extended interpretation of the work, as George and Martha in Albee's *Who's Afraid of Virginia Woolf?* may be seen as the primal husband and wife of the nation. The main characters in Shaw's *Man and Superman* parallel characters in Mozart's opera *Don Giovanni,* so that a comparison between the two works is necessary for a full insight into Shaw's intentions. Other names, like Blanche Du Bois and Stanley Kowalski in *A Streetcar Named Desire,* are associative. Others are suggestive, like the array of humorous names in Dickens' novels, which include Mr. Gradgrind, Mr. Bounderby, Mr. Murdstone, Mr. Pumblechook, Mr. Skimpole, and the Hon. Samuel Slumkey. Place names may take on the same qualities— *Streetcar* is set in a slum area of New Orleans called Elysian Fields—but names of this kind are usually not plentiful unless the work is clearly an allegory.

Equally important as the names chosen is the omission of names. Most of the soldiers in Stephen Crane's *The Red Badge of Courage* are nameless. It makes them as anonymous as soldiers become in a war; it also makes them universal. In a similar way, characters in Strindberg's *The Dream Play* are identified simply by their sex or occupation: He, She, The Daughter, The Officer, The Lawyer, The Poet. These are dreamlike figures; they are also universal types.

Allusions

Allusions represent the intricate interweaving of the author's reading and experience into his own writing. They are therefore a source of interest about the writer, but they may prove to be essential to a complete understanding of the work. An allusion like "Jonah's Moby" in a sonnet by Dylan Thomas is a kind of puzzle, but an entire poem based on an allusion, like Yeats's "Leda and the Swan," cannot be understood without knowing the mythological story. Frequently, a poet may give almost all of the facts one needs to know about an allusion, as Wallace Stevens in his poem "Peter Quince at the Clavier" tells the story of Susanna, taken from the Apochrypha; yet knowledge of the original story provides a base for knowing how Stevens uses the allusion for his own purposes. Literary references of this kind are clearcut; they can even be footnoted. But they do not cover all of the subtle echoes of phrase and line in a poem that may give clues to the author's thinking and meaning. In Eliot's *Murder in the Cathedral,* when the Second Priest expresses joy at the impending return of Archbishop Becket, the Third Priest says:

For good or ill, let the wheel turn.
The wheel has been still, these seven years, and no good.
For ill or good, let the wheel turn.
For who knows the end of good or evil?
Until the grinders cease
And the door shall be shut in the street,
And all the daughters of music shall be brought low.

The last three lines are almost the exact words of Ecclesiastes 12:3–4, and the first four lines suggest the spirit of Chapter 3 of the same book of the Bible. In this instance, the allusion is the meaning.

Allusions are obviously not limited to literary references. A major portion of Auden's "Musée des Beaux Arts" is based on a reference to Brueghel's painting of the fall of Icarus. His poem "September 1, 1939" is a topical allusion to the invasion of Poland by Hitler's troops. The allusion becomes the point of departure for the thoughts of the poem. It cannot be fully understood without that historical background. Allusions in writing are so very numerous that we can only conclude that the more we read and know, the more likely we will be able to come to grips with subtleties of meaning in an author's work.

Dialogue

One obvious source of ideas occurs in the dialogue of the characters. At times, when an author is interested in particular issues, he introduces a discussion among his characters. There seem to be no bounds—from general topics about morality, politics, and women's rights to more specific theories and ideas. Samuel Butler concerns himself with Darwinism in *The Way of All Flesh,* Dickens with Utilitarianism in *Hard Times,* and Shaw with the Bergsonian Life Force in *Man and Superman.* These sometimes take the form of actual intellectual discussion, sometimes influence the conception of the characters.

What one needs to guard against is to identify the views of a character in a novel or play with the author unless there is reason to do so. In a time when authors as self-advertisers are given to writing about their own ideas and their own works, identifications are often possible to make. Inevitably, a character who is a free-thinker or reformer becomes the author's mouthpiece. Some playwrights see themselves primarily as teachers or preachers. In the Epistle Dedicatory to *Man and Superman,* Shaw writes:

. . . it annoys me to see people comfortable when they ought to be uncomfortable: and I insist on making them think in order to bring them to conviction of sin. If you don't like my preaching you must lump it. I really cannot help it.

The ideas of a play, therefore, may be its main reason for its existence, and it becomes the interpreter's job to sort out opinions among the characters to see precisely how the ideas develop and how the action comments on them.

Extrinsic Sources of Thought

Thus far we have discussed the analysis of a literary work in terms of itself, in terms of the elements that combine to express meanings. This emphasis is sometimes referred to as formalistic; it has been more popularly labeled the New Criticism. What was new about New Criticism in the 1930s and 1940s has in one sense grown old, but it has now become established as an indispensable approach, particularly for the nonprofessional. What it does is assert the primacy of the text—it asks the reader to look at the text as material contained between the covers of the book and to consider it without reference to all of the other knowledge in the world that can be brought to bear on it.

However, the growing sterility of New Criticism, the social rebellion of the second part of this century, and a new spirit of Romanticism have brought about a shift in critical emphasis— from a consideration of the work as an isolated text, severed even from its author, to a consideration of the work in a variety of contexts. Thus, outside knowledge can be brought to bear on a literary work in such a way as to enlighten its meaning. These are extrinsic considerations. They are critical frames of reference that require specialized knowledge and are therefore less available to the amateur reader. Yet the perspectives which these approaches represent should be briefly considered.

Biographical Considerations

The biographical approach to literature is a standard one of long duration. Its value lies in the extent to which facts about the author's life help to clarify the content of his works. Its value also is relative. Some works contain more of their writers' immediate thoughts and experiences than others. If we had no outside sources of information about John Milton, for example, we would know most of the things we need to know about him from his own works. He constantly reflects on his own experiences in his prose and poetry and sometimes records them quite literally in personal digressions. On the other hand, the person of Shakespeare, about whom we know surprisingly little despite the fact that he is a major figure, cannot be inferred from the plays and poems. The biographies of him are based on a few facts and a mass of inference; they are largely speculative.

Biographical facts should not be absolutely necessary for reading a poem or story or play, but certainly all of the possible meanings have not been explored until they have been investigated. Once a work has been written, it is severed from its author, but the fact that it was derived from the source of his thought and experience may account for many things. The writer of biographical criticism needs to bear in mind one major caution: to keep the biographical facts and the critical interpretation in balance. When the life and works are discussed together, all too often the works are forgotten and the study becomes a biographical sketch. Biography is valuable as a study in its own right; it is not the same, however, as the critical application of biography to a work of literature.

Historical-Social-Political Considerations

Every literary work also springs from the context of its times. Yet, like the personal experiences of an author's life, these must be weighed more heavily in some works than in others for the obvious reason that some writers are more socially and politically conscious than others. The slavery issue and the Civil War are hardly reflected at all in the poetry of Longfellow; they are everywhere apparent in the poetry of Whitman. The French dramatist Giraudoux served in the Ministry of Foreign Affairs of France for a major portion of his life, eventually becoming the Minister of Propaganda, a post he held until the German occupation of France. His plays clearly show his interest in political matters.

Most writers at one point or another do make allusions to the times in which they live. What the writer does and what the critic does are two different things, however. What criticism of this variety tends to do is to read a particular work with a bias—to consider it as a political or social document and to consider it from the one view of history which the critic has adopted. Steinbeck's *The Grapes of Wrath* is a moving novel of human interest which can be read in terms of its own intrinsic values as a literary work; it is also an important social commentary on the plight of dispossessed farmers during the depression of the 1930s. In its sympathy with the farmer and its denunciation of the businessman, the work invites the attention of Marxist critics. For them, the analysis of the novel and also its values therefore hinge on the extent to which it is good or bad Marxist doctrine, on the extent to which the author seems to show attitudes of acceptance or rejection. The author's own intentions are in this case irrelevant. It is possible to read any author's work as Marxist if it is critical of materialism, religion, and traditional social values, although the author's own interests may not at all be political. Criticism of this nature often begins with presuppositions and then measures the literary work in terms of them. It imposes a framework on it. The critic becomes the spokesman, not the literary work itself.

Psychological Considerations

The difference between intrinsic and extrinsic considerations needs to be stressed constantly. It is one thing to examine the motivations of the characters in a novel; it is another to begin with a theory and to view all characters in terms of it. Or to take all of the outward signs of a character as symptoms of inner psychic drives so that a psychologist-critic can offer explanations not apparent to the nonspecialist. Criticism of this variety in a sense subjects literary characters or the author to psychoanalysis in terms of a particular school of thought. Freudian criticism is particularly common.

As fascinating as psychological criticism can be at times, its shortcomings should be apparent. The critic is limited to only what the literary work reveals—a selection of outward signs that cannot be expanded; he is unable to elicit more information from the subject. It is not surprising, therefore, that criticism of this kind tends to speculate, to fill in the gaps, to extend the meanings beyond those the work invites. The more complex a character is, the more likely he is to attract the attention of psychological critics. One of the standard works of this kind is Ernest Jones's study of Hamlet in terms of the Oedipus complex. Any writer whose works tend to dwell on introspection, sex, the macabre, the occult, the visionary, and the dreamlike—Poe, Kafka, Coleridge, and D. H. Lawrence come quickly to mind—is an especially fruitful source for this kind of critical analysis. Above all, however, criticism of this variety requires knowledge.

Archetypal and Mythic Considerations

Closely related to psychological criticism is an approach that views literature in terms of archetypal patterns and myths. This kind of criticism draws heavily on anthropology, religion, and mythology. It is an exploration of the communal response of all men to certain patterns of experience and phenomena of nature. These are inescapably a part of basic human behavior. For example, one of the archetypal experiences of all people is growth from childhood to adulthood, from immaturity to maturity, from innocence to knowledge. The pattern applies not only to individual experience but to collective experience as well. Thus, one of the best known of all myths, which like all myths may or may not have basis in fact, is the story of Adam and Eve in the Garden of Eden. Adam and Eve become primal father and mother. They are individuals; they are also all mankind. They pass from their state of innocence to a state of knowledge. As a result, they are expelled from Eden. Thus arises another deep subconscious drive in all men: the desire to return to the Edenic experience and the quest for a means, often a savior, to achieve it. In turn, other kinds of experience follow: suffering, sacrifice, and death, with the idea that these will achieve redemption, purification, and immortality. All of these human manifestations are reflected in the cycles of nature: all things spring to life, grow, die, and revive again. These patterns of nature and experience all men seem to know and understand and believe.

In ancient times, the archetypal patterns were embodied in simple but powerful stories that today we call myths. They are present in almost all cultures. Common motifs run through them, and they share symbols that are only variations on one another. Men are still fascinated with the simple mythic stories of the sun, moon, water, and the garden; or of a hero's search against obstacles for the answer to a riddle or a sword or a chalice which will make him a savior; or of a hero's willingness to die to deliver his people or remove the blight of sterility from the land.

These archetypal and mythic patterns continue to emerge in both the structure and imagery of contemporary writers. Critics interested in this approach are sometimes able to demonstrate convincingly that an author, whether intentionally or not, has once again recast one of the ancient myths in a new garb. These strains seem to demonstrate that beneath all of the knowledge and sophistication of modern man, he still cannot escape the most elemental concerns of his nature.

Like most of the extrinsic approaches, archetypal and mythic criticism requires an acquaintance with a vast body of knowledge on the subject. We may all know instinctively more than we think we know, but anthropology and cultural history provide a rich source of organized knowledge with which to begin.

Philosophical Considerations

It is not uncommon for authors to turn to philosophical works for clarification of their own thinking about the universe and to reflect this reading in their own works, sometimes superficially, sometimes profoundly. Therefore, an investigation of an author's own reading has been a fairly standard kind of project among scholars and critics interested in the influence of outside thought on a writer. One comes to understand Dante better by knowing Aquinas; Alexander Pope by knowing Deistic thought, which he got from his friend Bolingbroke; Wordsworth by knowing John Locke and David Hartley; John Stuart Mill by knowing Auguste Comte; and Shaw by knowing Henri Bergson. In more general terms, certain concepts occur over and over again in literature. Platonic ideas are pervasive in the writings of the Renaissance. The concept of the Great Chain of Being, which had its genesis in Greek philosophy, occurs again and again in philosophy and literature, as Arthur Lovejoy has shown in his book of the same name.

Knowing the philosophical backgrounds of a literary work can add immeasurably to one's understanding of it. The general reader should be aware, however, that the lack of this kind of outside knowledge does not necessarily present an insurmountable barrier toward understanding a writer. Authors also take on the role of informants. They often explain what they are talking about through one character or another. The purpose of criticism of this variety is finally to verify the accuracy of the writer's ideas and to see what adaptation he makes of other people's ideas for his own purposes. This type of analysis is a specialized approach which requires more than the capacity to name sources. If it is of value, it should add to the completeness of the work's meaning.

Considerations of Literary History

Criticism that involves literary history amounts to placing a writer or a particular work he has written into any number of literary contexts. An author can be considered in relation to a literary movement or he can be considered as influencing other writers or being influenced by them. A work can be considered as employing literary conventions or rebelling against them. A particular writer may be more important historically than the quality of his works justifies. Emile Zola is significant for his leadership of the Naturalistic movement in the late nineteenth century. His novels are still read, but they do not equal in reputation those of Stephen Crane, who followed later in the movement. John Lyly's *Euphues,* written in a highly inflated and affected style popular in the sixteenth century, gave the English language a new word, but the work ordinarily is known only through brief excerpts which appear in anthologies to illustrate "euphuism." Sarah Orne Jewett is an important writer of regionalist literature in America, but she has not achieved major stature as a literary figure. Gertrude Stein exercised a powerful influence on a whole group of writers and artists emerging in the 1920s, but many people find her own works largely unreadable. Thus, one can multiply the examples of literary figures and particular literary works that loom large in literary history, although they are not of major interest from other critical viewpoints. It is obvious that only an acquaintance with literary history can do justice to this form of criticism.

Creative Critical Responses

Another kind of critical response as an extrinsic source of thought may best be described as a bringing of the self to the literary work. It is creative rather than analytical; it is often an emotional response rather than an intellectual one. It requires only that the writer react in some way to the work he has read. He may want to imitate it; he may want to write a poem; he may be moved to give a personal testimonial to how he has responded to the work; he may want to speak to one of the characters. After reading Arna Bontemps' "A Summer Tragedy," one student wrote:

> I became so involved in the story that Bontemps could take me anywhere, have me see the story through any eyes. I could see where the people's outlook stopped and where the living situation began. Bontemps could inject any sensation into the story and I could feel it immediately.
> I am—no, it doesn't matter what I am except that I am a reader. Arna Bontemps is a writer. He reached me. He said his thing to me, I listened to him through my own patterns, and I saw thing his way all of a sudden. He made my world larger.

These are only the concluding remarks of a critical response which gives specific examples of why the writer was moved as she was. This is affective criticism, that is, criticism concerned with feeling. Like all highly personal criticism, it may say more about the student than about the work itself, but it does testify to the vital effect literature can have on the individual. Criticism does not need to be considered a purely diagnostic art; it can itself be a creative activity which seeks out its own forms and modes.

SUGGESTIONS FOR WRITING ABOUT
THOUGHT AND MEANING

Since thought and meaning emerge from almost all things that an author does in his composition, a few questions like the following help to bring into focus a large and involved topic:

1. To what extent is the author's meaning literal or metaphorical? Can the author's meaning be reduced to a sentence, or can it only be hinted at?
2. Is the author firmly committed to a point of view, or does he seem only to raise questions? Does he seem to express a particular philosophy or set of ideas which are peculiarly his own? Are the ideas derivative? Does the uncertainty about the author's meaning comment on the complexity of the work or on its purpose only to observe, not to give answers?
3. Does the title give a clue to the work's major emphasis? Does the work seem to be about other things than the title suggests? Is the title ambiguous? Is it derived from another source which will comment on the meaning of this work?
4. Do the names of characters and places seem to have special significance? Are they metaphorical? Associative? Allegorical? Are characters nameless for a particular purpose? Is any character an embodiment of an idea?
5. Are allusions a key to the author's meaning? Of what nature are they? Topical? Literary? Mythological? Natural? Is the allusion a passing reference or an integral part of the structure? What does a comparison with the source reveal about the author's use of it?
6. Do particular ideas dominate the dialogue? Are particular ideas countered by opposite views? What characters speak particular ideas? Are they sympathetic characters? Do they seem to speak for the author?
7. Are the ideas of a particular work dated? Have they been discredited by later findings and developments? Is the work therefore dated because its ideas are outmoded? Do some ideas seem to be perennial, unchanging?
8. What outside sources of knowledge does a particular work seem to invite? Is the work highly autobiographical so that the facts of the author's life are particularly relevant? Is it a work that concerns itself with a special body of knowledge so that full understanding depends on turning to outside sources? Is a special knowledge of psychology, philosophy, myth, or literary history particularly valuable?
9. What are the social and historical issues that will enlighten the meaning? Are they still vital considerations? Has the work transcended its own times?
10. What are the affective qualities of the meaning? How do you respond personally? Does the work anger you or sadden you? Are you in some way inspired? Why? What is the vital force of the work?

Writing on Literary Topics

General Approaches

The discussion up to this point has concentrated mainly on the nature of literature and the way it functions as an art form, indicating the kinds of things a reader can focus upon. With this as background, then, what can you do in actually writing about literature?

You Can Summarize

Summary statements are close to exercises that merely test the reader's capacity to paraphrase the content accurately. If you write a lengthy synopsis as a substitute for an essay, you should realize that you have done little more than given evidence that you have read closely enough to reproduce the details.

Summary may be considered the most elementary and least demanding approach to writing about literature. It does become important, however, when the presentation demands any kind of illustration. Even though you can often assume that your readers know the work under discussion, it is necessary to give brief summaries from time to time to refresh their memories and to establish a common base for understanding. When summary predominates over all other approaches, however, the readers know that you have failed to take the additional step of lending your own thought to the material.

You Can Interpret

Interpreting is seeing the implications of what is going on or what is being said in a literary work. It goes beyond retelling the story; it says what it is about. It may consist of any number of different approaches. It may mean deciphering the difficult syntax of a poem; it may mean recognizing that the reading of a poem is intentionally ambiguous and that it therefore has several implications. It may mean filling in the details of a story or play which are left implicit. By leaving some things unexplained, imaginative literature differs rather consistently from discursive prose. The essayist characteristically wants to supply as much detail as possible so that his meanings are direct and clear. But the writer of literature leaves much for the reader to conjecture and imagine. This is part of the appeal of literature.

Interpretation may also be described as translation as opposed to transcription. Nietzsche once wrote, "There are no facts, only interpretations." Once a work of literature is written, all kinds of private, representative, and universal implications may emerge. If a work by its obviousness or superficiality stimulates little thought, then there is little need for interpreting it. Interpretation may consist of working within the framework of the work itself—intrinsic considerations—in order to dig down into the core of meaning. Interpretation may also consist of extending outward —extrinsic considerations—in order to build on suggestions the literary work contains. In either case, interpretation amounts to bringing thought and feeling—your thought and feeling—to the act of reading and then verbalizing those thoughts.

Interpretation is seldom objective, but its subjectivity does not mean that it can be deliberately wrongheaded. When interpretation seems no longer to have any connection with the facts of the literary work, then surely it can be dismissed as farfetched. Interpretation consists of saying what you think, but saying what you think is one thing; saying what you think the writer is saying is another. As a writer and interpreter, you can think of yourself as an orchestral conductor who takes up the score of a musical work. You can make it your own composition by ignoring completely the author's intentions or you can put the composer first and let his leads bring out the fullest intentions of the work.

The best criticism makes the work primary; it begins with the work and keeps it always in focus. It is a critic's purpose to provide a number of access routes to understanding. If an interpretation leads the reader *to* the work, it provides a service. If it leads the reader completely *away* from the work, it has surely lost sight of its purpose as criticism.

You Can Analyze

Analysis is a kind of internal dissection that permits a reader to come to some understanding about the work as a whole. John Ruskin once defined artistic composition as "the help of everything in the picture by everything else." Analysis does assume that a literary work is organic, its parts working together to produce a total effect. It does not imply that the examination of the parts, like an exploratory operation of the human body, is done to discover what the flaws are. Analysis reveals weaknesses at times, but it may also increase the reader's understanding of how intricately the parts join together to cause us to respond as we do. Analysis is simply a way of seeking understanding.

Very often the secret of understanding is being able to ask good questions. The suggestions for writing about each of the components of literature given in the sections above furnish an array of questions for purposes of analysis and interpretation. One question—an obvious one—may provide only an obvious answer. Some readers know only obvious questions. If they ask a different question, a less obvious one, the answer may provide new insights. Above all, you must learn to ask your own questions.

The best criticism asks many different questions, although some critics who associate themselves with a particular school of thought may ask only a limited few. Thus they tend to see every literary work in the same terms. Their remarks become monotonous, pat, and often forced. Certainly as a student-critic you need all of the resources you can find, not only to be able to write about literature, but to form your own standards of critical judgment.

You Can Evaluate

To say of a literary work only "I like it" or "I don't like it" is not actually an evaluation; it is a dismissal. Personal response is an important beginning, but in some way it must be pushed further to say what the worth of a literary work is or what is lacking that would make it valuable. Evaluations, therefore, extend over a range of possibilities from formal considerations to private ones.

First, a work may be considered in terms of itself, as this book has emphasized. Evaluation of this kind assumes something about what a work of art should do, namely, that all of its parts should be working toward the total effect. Therefore, evaluation of this

kind asks how each part relates to the whole. And, equally important, how the parts relate to each other. Why do they follow one
another? What are the principles of arrangement? To say that a
literary work is "all of a piece" is in some way to account for
almost all of its details.

Although some literary works are not structurally flawless, they
are nevertheless impressive. Their worth may rest on other
grounds, perhaps on their plausibility: the plausibility of the
action, of the characters, of the thought. If the actions are contrived and improbable under the pretense of being lifelike, then
the illusion fails. If the characters are appealing but superficial,
then they may be wholly forgettable. Yet if the thought, though
fragmentary, is penetrating, the work may still have merit. The
elements of literature, however, are not ordinarily isolated from
one another. Evaluation is simply a way of considering the merits
and limitations of a work in separate terms.

A literary work may have worth in still other ways. Its value
may be judged in terms of its stylistic effectiveness—its use of
specific language and strategies. Criticism of this kind depends to a
great extent on reading experience, and comparison may be the
way of arriving at a decision about effectiveness. In one of his
critical essays on poetry, Matthew Arnold proposed that the best
way to determine excellence was "to have always in one's mind
lines and expressions of the great masters, and to apply them as
a touchstone to other poetry." He goes on to explain that other
poetry will not have to resemble these touchstones closely, but they
will serve as the means of determining the presence or absence of
quality. They are in a sense, then, reminders of what quality is.

Arnold's touchstone method can be easily discredited as too
intuitive, too limited, or too backward looking. Yet it does cause
us to ask ourselves what criteria we are using when we are moved
to praise. Some critics have no outside criteria; their decision
about worth depends on themselves alone.

Evaluation that depends wholly on your personal engagement
with a work is, of course, a private kind of criticism. You cannot
expect others to share your response unless you explain why you
feel as you do. That explanation may involve narrating a personal
experience which reveals why you have identified with a literary
work. You may show your involvement by recording your reactions in a journal. The form of the creative critical response may
be as varied as the individual who responds. Susan Sontag has
written, "What a few people know now is that there are ways of
thinking we don't yet know about. Nothing could be more important or precious than that knowledge, however unborn." Expres-

sive criticism may also be a source of thoughts yet unknown. You
need not shy away from it.

Formal considerations are essentially irrelevant to the final
judgments that expressive criticism makes, although an individual
who permits himself honestly to respond to literature may in time
become interested enough to ask himself what sources of value are
in the work itself when many other individuals find it equally
meaningful. Writing about literature is one way of discovering
what your own and other people's values are.

Specific Approaches

Finally, there is the matter of deciding what to write, how to focus
and develop the topic, and, then, always a hurdle to get over, how
to get started. Here are a few suggestions.

The Topic as an Aid to Writing

Writing about literature in the classroom often depends
on the topics assigned. In most instances, these are designed to help
you rather than hinder you and to focus your attention on matters that may not have occurred to you on your own. If the topic
is completely free choice, the demand is even greater because on
your own you must then know how to avoid the completely obvious.

In order to demonstrate the expectations and range of topics—
either those assigned or self-designed—a number of English instructors independently wrote assignments on a single literary
work, a modern one-act play by Dennis Jasudowicz entitled *Blood
Money*, described by the author as a play "on the value of money
stretching." The play is skeletal in form. It has only three characters: D.H., a Black man (the initials are those of D. H.
Lawrence), Lady C., a Black woman (the name suggests Lady
Chatterley, the main character of D. H. Lawrence's most famous
novel), and the Oil Magnate, unnamed, but described as an overfat
white man. The scene takes place in the mountains in a highly
grotesque cabin painted black with black window shutters. Recently, the Oil Magnate has sent a man to the slums to buy a
beautiful woman to bring to his mountain retreat, but when Lady
C. arrives he pays no attention to her. He has also brought a man,
D.H., to paint his cabin. D.H. and Lady C. are physically attracted to one another. When the Oil Magnate appears on the scene,
he speaks only the words "Gosh! Gosh!" and obscenely stuffs dollar
bills into his nostrils. D.H. and Lady C. defy Oil Magnate by
making love together outside the cabin as he listens inside. When

he will not readmit them to the warm cabin from the freezing outside, they taunt him. In the cold, they then grow desperate. D.H. first abuses Lady C. and then kills her in order to take for himself her warm clothes against the freezing weather. D.H. perishes in an avalanche of snow when he tries to sit on the roof of the cabin warming himself by the chimney. Oil Magnate remains inside, pinning two signs to the wall. One reads "HOME-COMING, I HAVE ARRIVED"; the other says "MESSIAH."

Each of the following topic assignments was written by a different instructor. Though each focuses on one element, in almost every case it is impossible to write about only one element of this play as if it were completely isolated from all of the other ones. If the topic focuses on character, it asks for the relationship between characters and thought; or if the topic focuses on language, it then speaks about language and strategy and purpose. The comments after each topic suggest what the instructor is trying to get you to see and do.

> 1. In *No Exit,* Sartre argues that "Hell is other people." A person's scheme of values is alien to others, and their schemes are alien to him. What causes the hell portrayed in *Blood Money*? Is it a conflict between white and black, rich and poor, man and man (that is, the "eternal triangle"), between individual schemes of value, or some combination? In other words, describe what seems to you to be the most significant cause for conflict. You would do well to make reference to actual statements in the play.

The topic begins with a definition drawn from another literary source and asks you to apply it to the situations in this play. This topic demands essentially an interpretation of the action, which, of course, cannot be separated from the characters who are involved in the conflict.

> 2. Which character in this play triumphs? You may take the position that in such a drama no one "triumphs," that "triumph" is a contradictory term. Whatever position you take, support it with evidence from the play. Keep in mind that the last figure on stage is not necessarily victorious, that the most interesting characters are not necessarily going to come out on top, that death is occasionally a triumph of sorts, and that your own sympathies, attitudes, and preferences have nothing to do with the outcome of the play.

This topic also deals with the conflict and its resolution. It asks who wins, if anyone does at all. In the assignment, the instructor tries to help you avoid obvious thinking on the subject and, finally, encourages you in this instance not to let your preconceptions get in the way of letting the play speak for itself.

> 3. The characters in this play form a triangle, a common device in

many stories of love and romance. Do the characters and the kinds of love they exhibit differ from those in other works with "love triangles" you have read? If so, in what ways?

This topic points to the pattern of characters in the play and then asks how the working out of the traditional triangle is different in this play from others of a more conventional nature. This topic, therefore, asks for internal analysis and the application of some outside information for purposes of comparison.

4. To the extent that these characters are not "real people," what do you suppose Jasudowicz's purposes are in working with "unreal people"?

This is a topic that actually asks about the nature and purpose of the special fictional universe that Jasudowicz has created. Since the play does not attempt to give an illusion of reality, you are asked to consider how this kind of approach comments significantly on life.

5. The Oil Magnate has no lines in the play. What other means does Jasudowicz use to characterize him?

This topic focuses on one character who is not revealed, as characters usually are, through spoken lines. The Oil Magnate says the words "Gosh! Gosh!" but he does not engage in dialogue. The topic therefore asks you to consider other nonverbal ways in which the nature of this character is made known.

6. Discuss the power and limitations of money in human relationships as suggested by the characters in *Blood Money*.

This topic asks for a discussion of the general idea of the play in terms of specific characters. The very fact that this topic is less focused than the others places a greater demand on you to limit it. You further have to caution yourself whether you are going to find yourself writing about how important money is in general or about how important money is as a factor in this play.

7. Does the play seem to present only a problem, or does it offer a solution; that is, does the play go anywhere?

This topic calls for an interpretation of the play as a whole, not in terms of the characters and actions but in terms of the general problem it treats. You must first decide what you consider to be the central thesis of the play and then consider whether the play merely makes observations or offers solutions and criticism.

8. There are several important threads in *Blood Money*. Choose one (for example, race, capitalism, Christianity, sex). Trace it through the play, and explore it in relation to what you see as the central theme.

This topic indicates that the previous question in number 7 does not necessarily ask for one right answer. There are several themes; this topic asks you to choose one and examine it as it is developed throughout the play. The assignment does not ask whether the play comes to solutions, but if you thought it did, you might appropriately discuss the ending.

> 9. Does the play submit to interpretation as a moral allegory? Consider especially whether good and evil are discussed in the play and, if so, what they embody.

This topic invites you to consider the play as a moral allegory. The characters, therefore, must be considered as embodiments of ideas and the conflict as a struggle between good and evil. You may find that the play does not fit such a simple pattern of moral allegory and argue accordingly.

> 10. Identify the elements in *Blood Money* that may be termed "absurd." How does the absurd function in the play? What effect does this absurdity have? Compare the use of absurdity in *Blood Money* with its function in "The Wrecker."

This topic focuses on dramatic strategy. You must consider why the playwright has chosen to introduce the obviously absurd elements. The assignment asks for interpretation and then for comparison with another work you have read in this particular class as a way of suggesting that the element of the absurd may not always have the same function.

> 11. Color—not only of skin—is used by the playwright, sometimes expressly, other times by implication, in developing his ideas. Focus on one major idea in the play and discuss how the colors help develop that idea.

This topic focuses on a different kind of strategy—the use of colors in the play as symbolical. You are asked to relate the color symbolism to the development of a particular idea. The theme, therefore, should not become merely a catalog or description; it must also be an interpretation.

> 12. Do you feel that the play's obscenity is overdone? Or do you feel that it bears a legitimate functional relationship to Jasudowicz's central concerns? Why or why not?

This topic asks you whether you think the play's language and situations accomplish what the playwright intends them to. As in most of the other topics, you have to come to some understanding of the play's meaning and then decide whether all things are working together to accomplish the writer's purpose.

13. There is an abundance of blood in this little drama. There is also a rich oil magnate who stuffs money in his nose. Comment on the possible significance of this action and try to develop an argument that relates the ideas of blood and money in the play. In other words, why is *Blood Money* a good title, if it is?

This topic assumes that the two key words of the title are especially important; it asks you to consider the action and ideas in terms of them and then to decide whether they are an adequate index to the action and thought in the play.

14. Study the language each person uses in the play and show how the speech of each helps to characterize him. Do their names and histories reinforce or conflict with your conclusions about their characters? If they conflict, what is the function of the contrast?

This topic asks for an analysis of the language as a device of characterization. If you choose to develop the question about the names and histories of the characters, you will have to turn to sources outside the play for information about D. H. Lawrence and Lady Chatterley. Without this knowledge, you will not be able to see a contrast.

15. Can you find a parallel between the ill-fated affair of D.H. and Lady C. and the Biblical story of Adam and Eve in the Garden of Eden? How does the recognition of such a similarity add to your understanding of the play?

This topic explores the possible mythic significance of the play. The whole issue would be whether this parallel adds significantly to your insight. If it did not, you obviously could not write at length on a topic like this one. See the student theme on this topic on p. 127.

16. Discuss the Oil Magnate in terms of his Messianic complex. In what ways is he or is he not a Messiah?

This topic also explores the mythic and psychological significance of the play in somewhat different terms. It also invites the possibility of considering the play as satire, since the play is clearly a distortion of any traditional myth.

17. Although most plays are written to be produced either on stage or in films, some are termed "closet dramas" because they are most suited for private reading and for some reason would not "come off" in production. Decide the category in which you think *Blood Money* belongs. Develop your argument with specific illustrations from the play.

This topic asks you to consider the theatrical possibilities of the play. Although some knowledge of the tradition of "closet drama" might be useful, it would not be absolutely necessary in order to indicate whether this play could be produced effectively or not.

> 18. One former student in this course complained that some of the anthology selections exhibited a "hang-up on sex a little outdated for today's young college student." He asked for selections which would express instead youth's "search for relationship and friendship with each other." Do you think this student would object to *Blood Money* on these grounds, or do you think the play expresses his concern for human relationship and friendship? Defend your opinion.

This is a topic that asks for a reaction to someone else's opinion about the play's relevance to current thinking. It involves an evaluation of the play not in terms of itself but in terms of personal standards.

> 19. Is this a moral play? If so, what moral lesson are we to learn and why? If it is not, why not?

This is a topic that also asks for an evaluation, but not in literary terms. The discussion would depend on your concept of what is moral and what isn't and your own response to this particular drama.

> 20. It could be claimed perhaps that the play with its violent language and simple plot works only because of its topical approach. But is the play purely topical, or does it appear to have some lasting value?

This is another kind of evaluation that is purely speculative: Does the play seem to have durable values? In a discussion of this kind, some knowledge of the literary tradition would be helpful, for example, a knowledge of what kind of work tends to fade and what kind tends to survive. The discussion demands a judgment and an opinion. If you are able to weigh the play's values, then you may also be able to estimate whether it has potential to transcend the change of time.

These topics on one short play—and they could be multiplied many times—suggest the range of emphasis that is possible in writing about literature. Of special importance is the fact that each topic has been phrased by someone who has already given the play careful thought. Each question hints, leads, or directs in some way. None forbids you to explore new possibilities, but each urges, shoves, lures you to think about what you may not have thought about before.

How To Focus and Develop

One of the main problems every writer has to solve is how to talk about a literary work as a whole without falling into vacuous generalizations. The problem increases as the length of the work increases, for the accumulation of detail seems always to invite a statement that will include the whole work. What happens can be illustrated by a sentence one student wrote in an attempt to cover three stories by D. H. Lawrence:

> In his three short stories, Lawrence deals with love relationships. He reveals the participants' feelings, needs, and desires—both conscious and unconscious—and their resulting behavior—emotional and often irrational—when these needs and desires are not fulfilled.

The weight of the generalization is almost more than one sentence can bear. But, more to the point, it is a high-level generalization that might apply to three stories by three other writers. It is not specifically a meaningful statement about the stories of D. H. Lawrence. How then can you avoid generalizing about all literature and all life so that an essay seems clearly related to the work it is discussing? How do you organize your thoughts so that in a relatively brief space you can indicate your grasp of the whole?

1. You can carefully select a speech or passage or detail that brings many elements of the work into focus. The discussion can then move outward to illustrate the central importance of this passage and its representativeness. The important emphasis here is to begin with the small significant detail and then develop more general thoughts.
2. Instead of the all too familiar summary theme that begins with the beginning, you can start with the end of the work and explain the outcome in terms of the earlier development. This approach invites selection of detail for purposes of illustration. In explaining why the work ends as it does, you often are led to explain the meaning of the whole thing.
3. You can attempt to see the major characters from the point of view of one of the secondary characters. This provides a means of selective analysis and demands an interpretation from a point of view other than the author's own. This approach provides fresh insight because we usually tend to focus on major characters. (Tom Stoppard's play *Rosencrantz and Guildenstern Are Dead* does this very thing. In this play, Hamlet is only a background character.)
4. You can collect small clues and signs that set the tone and create an atmosphere for the whole work. Here you can often be original because you may be sensitive to details that others do not see.
5. You can select one theme for discussion rather than the full breadth of the literary work. This suggestion may also permit

you to pursue a personal interest. For instance, you may see chauvinism in the speeches of the men characters, even though the main theme of the play does not concern women's rights.

6. You can attempt to relate selected details of the story to a single emotional effect: one work as a study in horror, another as a study in the grotesque, another as dreamlike.

7. You can examine particular literary devices as a way of discovering how the author creates his effects. You, of course, need to know what a literary device is. This book has attempted to explain how literature works through form, language, character, plot, style, and setting.

8. You can begin with what interests you most about the work and then try to account for this reaction in terms of other things that have receded in your attention. How finally does everything fit together?

9. You can begin with an interpretation or critical evaluation written by someone else and then agree or disagree, support or refute, expand or offer an alternate interpretation. This approach requires some outside reading. It has its advantages and disadvantages. You can always learn from others, to be sure, but you want to make certain that you do not use outside criticism as a crutch or, even worse, as a substitute for your own thinking.

10. Instead of writing directly about the work, you can attempt to do a creative piece of your own that either expresses your response to the work you have read (see essay on p. 132) or gives the work a modern or personal setting so that your understanding of the original is fully revealed (see story on p. 133).

How To Get Started

Each of the student themes that follow illustrates a way of beginning. In order, the nine themes begin as follows:

1. This theme begins with an evaluation and then attempts to support that judgment.
2. This theme begins with a condensed sketch of the character to be discussed.
3. This theme begins with a statement of personal feelings that relate to the work.
4. This theme begins with a quotation.
5. This theme begins with a broad generalization, then narrows it to the work being discussed.

6. This theme begins with two questions that attempt to get at the central meaning of the poem.
7. This theme begins with a comparison that will be more fully developed.
8. This theme begins with a personal narrative.
9. This theme, a story, begins with an important statement of fact.

These particular beginnings are in each instance appropriate to the approaches used in those essays.

Even when students are assigned the same topic, they choose different focuses and organization and thus come up with different beginnings. The following students, after having read Philip Roth's *Goodbye, Columbus,* were asked to describe the world of that novella—the fictional universe Roth creates. They could focus on any character or on any group of characters. Here are five examples:

> The world of *Goodbye, Columbus* is one of hot summer days, the smell of fresh-cut grass, and two people discovering the meaning of love. Neil Klugman and Brenda Patimkin come from different worlds, but as their relationship evolves, they form their own separate world in which their lives and love coexist. Their "special" world overlaps with the personal worlds that their families and friends are part of.
>
> • • •
>
> *Goodbye, Columbus* deals with Neil Klugman, a middle-class Jew, college graduate, and library employee, who falls for Brenda Patimkin, college student, Jewish, from a wealthy family. They have an affair one summer which comes to a bad end in the fall. So much for the introduction.
>
> The world created in *Goodbye, Columbus* was formed by a fusion of the two different worlds of Neil and Brenda. The world which existed between these two people did not last, for it was not a real world at all. It was closer to never-never land.
>
> • • •
>
> Brenda's world in *Goodbye, Columbus* consisted of her glasses, a jealous mother, an adoring father, a typical, spoiled little sister, a collegiate athlete, a Black maid, Radcliffe, an empty temple, three hundred dollars that used to be in an old sofa, an old refrigerator full of fruit, a sports tree, a Chrysler and a Volkswagen, and an ego-builder called Neil Klugman.
>
> Her world is a storybook ideal that every little girl dreams of acquiring. . . .
>
> • • •
>
> The little Black boy in *Goodbye, Columbus* lives in a world of fantasy. It is so much more appealing to him than the environment that surrounds him. His fantasy world is present only at the library.
>
> • • •
>
> The worlds of the individual characters in *Goodbye, Columbus* are

so different in terms of values and priorities that it is impossible for them to blend into one, and therein lies the conflict of the story.

The world of Neil Klugman is shaped by a middle-class upbringing in Newark, New Jersey. [details follow]

Things have always come easy for Brenda. [details follow]

So we have Brenda and Neil escaping from their own worlds. They find it impossible, however, to make one world acceptable to them both. . . .

The final example indicates in skeleton form the beginning, the development, and the ending of the whole theme. Once a beginning has been determined—a thesis—and some sense of direction has been given, then almost all of the remainder of such an essay is expansion by way of illustration. How this development is worked out completely can be seen in the student essays that follow.

Student Examples

1. WRITING ABOUT FICTION: A CRITICAL EVALUATION

"Go Down, Moses"—The Old versus The New

The most successful story in Faulkner's *Go Down, Moses* is the final episode entitled "Go Down, Moses." This story is successful because it achieves, in a simple way, the presentation of the attitudes and misunderstandings which are part of the southern heritage. The story revolves around Mollie Beauchamp, a post-Civil War Negro, and Gavin Stevens, the county attorney. Mollie represents the old order of Negro society which is incapable of handling its own affairs after two centuries of slavery, and Gavin Stevens represents a segment of the modern white society that knows it must live with the Negroes and senses an obligation toward them. This obligation is unusual, or perhaps it may be said to be traditional in the same sense that the pre-Civil War plantation owner had an obligation to his slaves. Yet, Gavin Stevens does feel a respect and compassion for the downtrodden Negroes. This story attempts to determine the extent of the obligation of one race to the other, at least as it is resolved in one man's mind.

The story also probes the questions, How much is a "dead nigger" worth to the white race and ultimately how much is the entire Negro race worth to the white race? The story is successful because of the way Faulkner arrives at his answers. He sets up a situation in which Mollie's boy has disappeared. She believes that he is in trouble and goes to the county attorney for help. The bulk of the story is concerned with the county attorney's efforts to ease Mollie's burden. In the course of the action, the reader draws several conclusions relevant to southern life and thinking:

1. Mollie and a majority of the southern Negroes do not and probably will not understand completely the system of white domination in which they must function.
2. The white race still does not understand the Negro's thinking and emotional patterns.
3. The Negro is still treated as a child by the white race as a result of the two races' misunderstandings.
4. There is no immediate solution to the problems between the races.

Yet, why is this story unique? True, Faulkner has explored these same conflicts in other stories, but he has nowhere else crystallized them as he does in the final story of *Go Down, Moses.* He has gotten away from the plantation, where white domination is traditionally expected; he has gotten away from the hunt, where all men tend to be equal in the chase; and in this story he has situated himself in the city, the new center of southern life in the years after the Civil War as Negroes drifted from the plantations. He has shown how the same attitudes, prejudices, and misunderstandings that he has so carefully explored in the earlier stories now function in the city, in the new restructured social system.

This story, with the possible exception of "The Bear," is the most vital in the entire collection, as Faulkner is pitting the old social order against modern society and new situations. He is not simply explaining life on the plantation with its predictable patterns of behavior, but life in the modern world where action does not allow a predictable pattern. It is this unpredictable pattern—that Stevens goes so far out of his way to please the mother of a dead Negro, who to him is only a criminal—that makes this story unique.

Stevens realizes that the whites have an obligation to the Negroes, not as the McCaslins did because they owned them as slaves but because the Negroes are people with desires and feelings the same as any member of the white race. Faulkner's characters do not reach this point of understanding in any of the other stories. "Go Down, Moses" is successful because it explores the old relationships in contrast with the new and thus gives us a new perspective on southern life that none of the other stories can provide.

Comment The essay begins with an evaluation: the writer's judgment that one particular story in a collection is the most successful of the group because it accomplishes effectively what it sets out to do. The writer immediately begins summary details as a way of justifying the conclusions that follow. The summary naturally involves the characters, action, and setting; the conclusions are the emerging ideas. In an effort to establish the uniqueness and success of this particular story, the writer then turns to comparison. He says that the setting of this story makes it unique. He refers also to its special vitality and to the depth of its understanding and penetration. Each of these points he attempts to support.

In the course of the analysis, the writer has touched on most of the elements of fiction except possibly the style. Even so, there is some concern with tone. The essay indicates clearly how summary, analysis, interpretation, and evaluation depend on one another and how the various components of this story cannot be rigidly separated from one another for purposes of writing.

2. WRITING ABOUT FICTION: A CHARACTER ANALYSIS

Hulga's Lesson

In Flannery O'Connor's "Good Country People," Hulga Hopewell learns a lesson that her Ph.D. in philosophy did not prepare her for. When we are first introduced to the stout, thirty-two-year-old woman who has a wooden leg as a result of a childhood accident, her emotional sterility and lack of sensuousness are sharply contrasted with the sexuality of Glynese and Carramae. Their mother, Mrs. Freeman, supplies an intensely physical and sexual background by detailing the girls' bodily functions and ailments.

Hulga, of course, is disdainful of such banalities and seems intent on denying that such matters are important. Instead, she cultivates her ugliness so that she will not have to compete with the Glyneses and Carramaes of the world. She lumbers around the house in her sweatshirt with the faded cowboy on it, exaggerating her deformity and feeling continuous outrage. At thirty-two, she has never danced, never been kissed, and, in her mother's terms, has never had "any *normal* good times." Instead, she reads philosophy. Ironically, because of a bad heart, Hulga lives at home on her mother's farm, surrounded by the unsophisticated and earthy people—the good country people—she scorns.

Hulga is particularly proud that, without telling her mother in advance, she had her name legally changed from Joy to Hulga, a name that Mrs. Hopewell thought must be "the ugliest name in any language." Hulga saw it as "her highest creative act. One of her major triumphs was that her mother had not been able to turn her dust into Joy, but the greater one was that she had been able to turn it herself into Hulga." But, for all of her pride, Hulga has not succeeded in becoming indifferent to her deformity; she is preoccupied with it, intent upon proving an indifference that is disproved by the very intent. Because she cannot admit to herself that she is infirm, she tries to make herself into something else, into Hulga. Thereby, she will seem to be in control of her condition, to have willed herself to be deformed as a jesting reply to the "normal" people around her. She even treasures her deformity and suffering for making her different. She is highly sensitive about both her wooden leg and her adopted name, for they are very personal matters, important to her as psychological symbols. In fact, she fancifully, yet quite seriously, attributes special powers to her new name and the self-willed ugliness it represents: "She had a vision of the name working like the ugly sweating Vulcan who stayed in the furnace and to whom, presumably, the goddess had come when called."

Because Hulga realizes that the people around her are often foolishly conventional in their ideas and values, she deceives herself that she lives with no illusions. Her illusions are only more sophisticated than theirs. Her claim that there is "nothing to see" means merely that she does not find anything to see, not that "nothing" can be the object of symbolic insight. In one of her books, Hulga has underlined a passage: "Nothing—how can it be for science anything but a horror and a phantasm? If science is right, then one thing stands firm: science wishes to know nothing of nothing. Such is after all the strictly scientific approach to Nothing. We know it by wishing to know nothing of Nothing." To Mrs. Hopewell, such words were gibberish, but to Hulga they were an "evil incantation" to ward off the experience of nothing. Hulga remains emotionally safe because she, too, wishes to know nothing of nothing. Her philosophical position is nonsensical, for it has developed out of neurotic needs, her need to escape her socially and physically incomplete self, her dread of nothing, and her realization that she is dust like all mankind. So she becomes a ridiculous case of a satirist satirized or a rationalist revealed as irrational.

Hulga is equally absurd when she sets out to enlighten an apparently naive Bible salesman, an action she thinks is objectively experimental and in his best interests. Her motives are actually selfish. She clearly wants to disillusion the young man to demonstrate her superiority, to recreate him as she thinks she has recreated herself. She wants to continue her defensive attack on the good country people. Yet her plan for his philosophical education reveals perhaps even more repressed motives. She intends to seduce him and then lead him to realize that there is nothing to see: "She imagined that she took his remorse in hand and changed it into a deeper understanding in life. She took all his shame away and turned it into something useful."

The murkiness of Hulga's motives and her lack of self-knowledge make her vulnerable to the counterfeit country bumpkin; in fact, she even considers running away with him. In the first place, she is moved that the young fellow sees "the truth about her," since he claims that her wooden leg makes her different from everyone else. She does not realize that he is even more of a morbid fetishist than she is. She even imagines that, after they have run away together, "every night he would take the leg off and every morning put it back on again," a fantasy that suggests her neurotically elevated sexuality, her secret desire to relax her defenses, and her need to admit dependence.

The climax of the story is a violent attack on Hulga's illusions. As the Bible salesman drops his disguise as "good country people," he reveals that he is more cynical than she, that his sexual attitudes toward her are brutal and obscene. And, most importantly, his belief in nothing is far more radical than hers. When Hulga was faced with what seemed to be an adoring, childlike boy, she felt safe enough to experience emotions that she had previously protected herself against. When she is faced with a diabolical nihilist who changes his name at every house he visits and has been "believing in nothing ever since I was born," Hulga is exposed as an adolescent by comparison. Having been emotionally and psychologically seduced, Hulga is the one who is educated. For the first time she is forced to "see through to nothing," an experience far less comfortable than she had imagined. As she is abandoned by the salesman, left in a state of shock without her glasses and her wooden leg and her feigned self-sufficiency, her old self has been destroyed. She may be forced to make a new beginning. Perhaps it may even lead her to accept her own body with its deformity and sexual desire, to accept the ironies inherent in man's spiritual and bodily nature.

  Comment On the most superficial level, the story of Hulga Hopewell might be seen as merely a seduction of a naive woman by a sinister man, another popular magazine story. But, of course, it is not that at all, and this student essay tries to probe the psychological and philosophical dimensions of the story and to establish that the simple plot involves an interaction between highly complex characters. Hulga, however, is the main focus. The other characters of the story are introduced only to the extent that they contribute to an understanding of her.

If paragraph four of the essay is not as clear as it might be in its explanation, the student must still be admired for tackling, not evading, the intellectual challenge of a difficult passage. The essay should be especially commended for its full use of supporting evidence and for smoothly integrated quotations.

3. WRITING ABOUT FICTION: AN IMPRESSIONISTIC COMPARISON

On Seeing a Blind Bird

There is something about seeing the blind that wrenches horror out of the viewer. Perhaps it is an innate fear in us that we, too, may be blind one day. Or maybe it is an instinctive aversion to weakness. Certainly our immediate reaction to blindness is not sympathy. Every fiber in us resists the humane attitude.

This horrified fascination hits a viewer of "Blind Bird," a black-and-white ink painting by Morris Graves. Graves's bird, black and huddled, clings flightless to a rock, its feet bound down by a tangle of white cobwebs. The bird's eyes are either dark voids or nonexistent. It crouches alone; it touches nothing but its rock, the tangle holding it there, gray mists around it, and whatever its mind contains. The bird looks totally vulnerable, yet somehow utterly impenetrable.

The main character in Dostoevsky's "Notes from Underground" draws from the reader that same "Blind Bird" horror. We may ultimately wring a drop of pity from our hearts over the underground man's plight if we feel no identity with him, yet immediately we feel a revulsion over his condition. The underground man seems to huddle bitterly in his shell as the bird does on its rock, bound to his spot with a web of uncontrollable thought patterns. He broods like the bird; what else can a vulnerable flightless hulk do?

Something about blindness urges us to ask, "How did this happen?" The question is usually not derived from kind concern but rather from a certain morbid curiosity. There is more than a hint of lingering Puritanism in our unvoiced suspicion that somehow the blindness is a result of the afflicted creature's actions: perhaps the bird might still see if it had been a good bird; perhaps the underground man would be a social success if he did not cling so obstinately to his bizarre reflections.

The lingering quality of the "Blind Bird" is a certainty of unalterable isolation. The bird will not enjoy voluntary solitude; the webby tangles imprisoning its feet will keep it on its rock in a most involuntary manner. Yet if the bird had a chance to fly, we can suspect it would react just as the underground man says:

> Come, try, give any one of us . . . a little more independence, untie our hands, . . . relax the control and we . . . yes, I assure you . . . we should be begging to be under control again at once.

Comment This essay is an attempt to solve the very difficult matter of expressing one's feelings about a work of literature in such a way that another reader will understand what the effect has been on the writer. With an opening paragraph about human reactions to blindness in general, the writer turns immediately to a painting by Morris Graves. Not until the third paragraph do we come to the literary work under discussion, but the previous remarks have prepared the reader for a meaningful comparison. From that point on, the thought vacillates back and forth from bird to man and from man to bird. The writer has made the two one.

4. WRITING ABOUT DRAMA: ANALYSIS AND INTERPRETATION

The Hope of Man

"Think of living up there in the top flat, with a beautiful young wife, two pretty little children and an income of twenty thousand crowns a year," yearns The Student in the first scene of Strindberg's *The Ghost Sonata*. To live in a house like that would be the answer to his hopes for happiness. His hope is for a life of sweet, innocent love, of sunshine-filled rooms with pink draperies, of his own children's bubbling laughter, and of money enough to insulate himself from the common worries of existence. This is his personal interpretation of the basic hope of man—that somewhere there is something beautiful and true to make the suffering of life worthwhile. The question asked by The Girl—so often asked but so seldom answered—is therefore central: "Is life worth so much hardship?"

Strindberg's *The Ghost Sonata* is not a play written to fill one's heart with hope for human triumph over the "labor of keeping the dirt of life at a distance," as the girl aptly phrases the problem. Instead, Strindberg destroys the false dreams of the romantic and, through a horror-filled nightmare, shows the blackness of reality that is hidden so securely behind a well-scrubbed facade of deceit. This is shown symbolically by the house—modern, pleasant-appearing, so seemingly filled with "beauty and elegance." It is a mansion. To the passerby it is the home of virtuous and high-minded aristocrats: the wealthy colonel, the benevolent consul, the aged spinster, the baron, the beautiful daughter, and the well-mannered servants. But what are these people after Mr. Hummel, the most flagrant deceiver of them all, disrupts their stagnating existence, and "the deepest secret is divulged—the mask torn from the imposter, the villain exposed . . ."? All of these people are tortured by the sins of their past; all live on in the horrid loneliness of a hell full of "crime and deceit and falseness of every kind," in which payment is painfully wrung from their condemned souls.

In this symbolic house of lies, what is more a paradox of appearance and reality than the Hyacinth Room, full of the splendor of nature? The Student extols hyacinths of many colors: "the snow-white, pure as innocence, the yellow honey-sweet, the youthful pink, the ripe red, but best of all the blue—the dewy blue, deep-eyed and full of faith." But The Girl shows the other side of the picture: "This room is called the room of ordeals. It looks beautiful, but it is full of defects." The chimney smokes, the desk wobbles, the pen leaks, the maid makes more work for the girl, the cook gives her no nutrition. "Living is hard work, and sometimes I grow tired," laments The Girl. Finally, she grows tired from her labors and dies. Her whole life is a hopeless situation; for, as the student explains, "The very lifespring within you is sick."

There is no hope here for The Girl, or for man in general. But is there hope in the patient Buddha, waiting endlessly for the time when "this poor earth will become a heaven"? I think not. The Student explains, "Buddha sits holding the earthbulb, his eyes brooding as he watches it grow, outward and upward, transforming itself into a heaven." This symbol of man's hopes seems to be contradicted by the meaningless death of the girl, killed by the world's cruel deceit. Buddha's shallot, blooming beautifully out of the ugly earth, is the hope of man. Yet it may be contrasted with another flower, the girl, the flower of reality, who withers and dies in this vale of tears we call life.

To end the play, The Student soliloquizes on the hopelessness of finding anything in life worth living for. He hopes that death will liberate, that the girl will eventually find the hopes of man fulfilled "by a sun that does not burn, in a home without dust, by friends without stain, by a love without flaw."

Comment The clarity and orderliness of this analysis belie what a remarkable accomplishment this short essay is. The student takes a highly complex, symbolical drama and by focusing on selected details of the setting and dialogue by two of the main characters manages to get at the substance of Strindberg's thought. At no point does he summarize the action, although he does suggest in paragraph two what the general situation is. He is primarily concerned with the strategies that Strindberg uses: the house, the Hyacinth Room in particular, the Buddha. All of these he interprets so that their significance is made known. But the essay is not all formalistic analysis. When the major topic of the paper—the hope of man—is introduced in the fourth paragraph, the writer expresses his personal opinion. He shares the doubts of the student in the play. He makes clear which character he identifies with.

5. WRITING ABOUT DRAMA: A MYTHIC INTERPRETATION AND PERSONAL ASSESSMENT

Blood Money

Often in modern plays the author creates characters that are concerned with a major problem, but, unlike plays from past centuries that conclude with a moral being learned or a lesson taught, these modern plays generally leave the reader in a state of wonder, not knowing answers, forced to decide for himself. One such play is *Blood Money* by Dennis Jasudowicz. The author presents a problem, but has left the decision-making to the reader: which character is the hero, which is right in his actions, which to believe, what to think.

The love between D.H. and Lady C. resembles the Biblical story of Adam and Eve—lovers in the ideal state who have sinned and are forced to face the consequences of their sin. D.H. and Lady C. willingly sin and realize too late that it means the loss of their re-entry to the paradise of safety, warmth, and shelter. The god they have spurned, the power above them (represented by the Oil Magnate) now spurns them and is deaf to their cries and pleadings. Their faith in each other is destroyed as they realize their situation—that they have caused their own downfall in mistakenly believing and having faith that they will be forgiven.

Faith, here, is an extremely important issue. Do I trust and have faith in those I love, in those who have power over me, or only in myself? In *Blood Money* all these possibilities seem to be ridiculous, since we must watch as Lady C. is murdered by her trusted lover, as the powerful Oil Magnate shows no mercy toward the lesser beings, and as D.H.'s faith in himself is destroyed.

The author has touched on the timeless search of every age. Is it enough to have myself, have faith that I can survive and succeed? Or is it necessary to find another to love, to rely on someone else besides myself for security, happiness, and success? Or are these relationships too concrete and too earthly? By this I mean, does man have to go out of his own personal realm towards faith in and love for a superior being with power over him? Man in himself is so small, but added to another is twice again in size. D.H. and Lady C. could have had so much strength and beauty in their love and unity, but the weak basic nature of man allowed fear and desperation to take the upper hand. Man can add nothing to himself with false relationships; only through honesty and truth can strength and success in friendship and love grow. Perhaps man's belief in a superior being is his only hope, perhaps it is his major downfall. I have yet to come to a decision. . . .

Comment This essay begins by stating that *Blood Money* is the kind of play that leaves moral decisions to the reader. This student does not have moral preconceptions which will simplify looking at the play. The essay is an attempt to consider the possibilities, to ask questions.

The interpretation begins by rather remarkably condensing into one paragraph a parallel between the Garden of Eden story and the situation in *Blood Money*. This comparison then invites the possible solutions to man's plight: faith and love. A kind of self-examination follows, but the answers are prompted by details from the play. At this point, the student has not abandoned the drama to write a personal narrative. The essay reveals the student's mind at work in interaction with the play. The essay concerns itself primarily with the plot and the ideas that grow out of it.

6. WRITING ABOUT A POEM: ANALYSIS AND INTERPRETATION

Organization: A Definition

Anecdote of the Jar

I placed a jar in Tennessee,
And round it was, upon a hill.
It made the slovenly wilderness
Surround that hill.

The wilderness rose up to it,
And sprawled around, no longer wild.
The jar was round upon the ground
And tall and of a port in air.

It took dominion everywhere.
The jar was gray and bare.
It did not give of bird or bush,
Like nothing else in Tennessee.
—Wallace Stevens

If there were no black, would white have meaning? If there were no night, what would day mean? It is this basic premise—that a concept has no meaning, or substance, until it is contrasted with an opposite concept —that seems to prompt Wallace Stevens to write "Anecdote of the Jar." The poem is a contrast between jar and wilderness, exemplifying a dependency of jar and wilderness on each other for definition. The jar lends substance to the wilderness, just as the wilderness defines the jar.

Consider the man who, traveling through a presumably unexplored region, comes upon a beer bottle in the midst of it. Not only does he feel a sense of depression at discovering that the region is not unknown but he also is struck by the contrast between bottle and wilderness, or in a broader sense, between that which is man-made and that which is not. In "Anecdote of the Jar" the jar is placed deliberately upon nature by man, perhaps as an experiment, to judge the effect of art on nature. The poem itself is an account, an observation of the contrast it creates.

The jar is "round," suggesting a sense of structured order, but the wilderness is "slovenly" and "sprawled around," portraying a lack of neatness and organization. The jar assumes superiority over the wilderness. It "made" the wilderness surround the hill. It causes the wilderness to "rise" up to it, an image which also supports the idea that the jar is above the wilderness, not only physically but hierarchically. It tames the wilderness until it is "no longer wild"; it is "sprawled around," implying a sense of subservience. The jar is "tall and of a port in air," a note of the jar's height and an observation of its noticeability.

The jar stands out in an unnoticed wilderness, and in this way, the jar grants dimension to the wilderness. Without the jar there is no criterion for judging any aspect of the wilderness. By providing contrast, it is also defining the area, as black defines white.

The idea of the jar's superiority is repeated in the third stanza: "It took dominion everywhere." Man claims no dominion over nature, because he himself is created as wilderness is. But, by means of the jar, man is able to organize wilderness, and in this way, wilderness falls into the order of man. This organized, ordered structure causes wilderness to appear "slovenly" and unstructured, through force of contrast, creating a similar effect to that which one obtains from pondering the question of life's meaning in the absence of death.

The jar is an artifact—a man-made product. It is a functional thing, but it is also unproductive. It is "gray and bare" and does not "give of bird or bush." And so, though the jar can organize and grant definition to wilderness, it cannot produce life. To me, in brief, the poem contrasts man's creativity and nature's. The jar, being man-made, follows a human organization. The wilderness does not; yet it can produce "bird and bush" —life, the most organized structure of all. The jar cannot.

Comment Since the Stevens poem is short, the paper attempts to deal with the complete meaning and purpose; it does not touch on other elements of the poem at all. The first paragraph states the basic premise that the essay will develop. It is the student's interpretation of the meaning; it is the conclusion he has come to after his careful reading, which the remainder of the essay suggests. Paragraph two offers an analogy. If the experience of the poem seems somewhat abstract and remote, this example makes it familiar. Paragraphs three and four of the essay proceed line by line through the first two stanzas of the poem, selecting details and relating them to the main idea of the poem. Paragraphs five and six develop the thought further in terms of the third stanza, constantly phrasing and rephrasing the basic premise. Interpretation throughout is the product of analysis. It is the kind of poem that can be defined in this way.

7. WRITING ABOUT A POEM: A SOURCE STUDY AND COMPARISON

The Journey of the Magi

"Journey of the Magi" by T. S. Eliot tells about the three Wise Men and their visit to the newborn child Jesus. Although the poem is based on the familiar Biblical story written by Matthew, Eliot's version presents a decidedly different view. In the Bible, Matthew tells these things about the Magi:

> Now, when Jesus was born in Bethlehem of Judaea in the days of Herod the king, behold, there came wise men from the east to Jerusalem, saying, "Where is he that is born King of the Jews? for we have seen his star in the east, and are come to worship him." . . . When they had heard the king, they departed; and, lo, the star, which they saw in the east, went before them, till it came and stood over where the young child was. When they saw the star, they rejoiced with exceeding great joy. And when they were come into the house, they saw the young child with Mary his mother, and fell down, and worshipped him: and when they had opened their treasures, they presented unto him gifts; gold, and frankincense, and myrrh. And being warned of God in a dream that they should not return to Herod, they departed into their own country another way.
> —Matthew 2:1, 9–12

Matthew's recounting of the story deals with the journey in a very few words. His is less of a story than a direct narration of facts. He skips over the actual details of the journey, simply saying that the Wise Men "went their way." The main emphasis of his view of the journey is on the moment when the Magi see Jesus. Matthew stresses their worship and rejoicing, and their offerings of precious gifts. Of utmost importance in the Biblical version are the joy and humility of the great Wise Men before Jesus, whose worship of him shows the importance of Jesus. The return of the Magi and the outcome of their visit, much like their original journey, is ignored by Matthew. Once the Magi leave Bethlehem and Jesus, Matthew's interest in them fades, and he states simply: "they went back to their own country."

In telling the same story as Matthew, T. S. Eliot depicts the events quite differently. In great contrast to the Biblical version, Eliot's poem skips over the actual moment when the Magi reach Jesus and his mother. In a monumental understatement, Eliot's Magi state: "it was (you may say) satisfactory." Clearly what is important in the poem is not the circumstances of the meeting itself, but how the Birth affects the Magi before and after they are confronted with it.

Eliot places great emphasis on the details of the journey. He aptly portrays what an ordeal the journey must have been, a journey undertaken at the very "worst time of year," in the "very dead of winter." He stresses the cold, sharp weather, the length of the journey, and the soreness of the camels. He tells of people hostile and unfriendly, going about their careless ways in spite of the great event taking place in Bethlehem. Underneath it all is the great doubt of the Magi, wondering if the destination is worth the ordeal of the journey: "With the voices singing in our ears, saying that this was all folly."

The poem, differing from the Bible, also contains details about the arrival of the Magi in the "temperate valley." They see "a running stream and a water-mill beating darkness," suggesting that growth and thriving life are here conquering darkness. With Jesus' birth, hope is born. Contrasted with these signs of birth and hope are images that the Magi see about the countryside, images recalling death. The "three trees on the low sky" recall the three crosses on Golgotha, and the men in the tavern are at an open door "dicing for pieces of silver," just as men drew lots for Jesus' clothes before he died.

The outcome of the journey, totally ignored by Matthew, is seriously dealt with by Eliot in his poem. He describes how the Magi return to their kingdoms but are not at ease. In losing their ignorance of what is truly right, they have lost their "old dispensation" to lead lives of corruption. They realize that their old life cannot suffice for them any longer. Thus, the Birth is their "death" in that it makes them reject the lives that they had once led. In saying this, Eliot is talking about another "journey," that of the struggle they will have to change their lives completely. His description of the new journey parallels the old. The Magi are confronted with severe hardships; their people are alien to them, clutching "gods" instead of the one true God that the Magi have witnessed. Their new realizations, in the form of the Birth, are "hard and bitter agony" for them. In their first journey they "at times regretted" going; likewise, in the second they "should be glad of another death." What is important is that in both journeys, on the way to Bethlehem and on the way to making a new life for themselves, they overcome their doubts and follow the road that they, despite their misgivings, know to be right.

Because the poem fully explores the journey of the Magi, Eliot's version of the story is infinitely more meaningful than Matthew's simple narration of the events. "Journey of the Magi" carries a special impact because it dramatizes the force and the outcome of the events that Matthew merely describes.

Comment The productiveness of this essay springs from the fact that the student has returned to the source from which the story of the Magi is taken and has indicated how the two accounts differ in their interests. By comparing, she is able to see what Eliot has added in his poem and how the additions say something new, not inconsistent with Christian doctrine but a further illustration of it. Eliot has focused his story-poem on the minor characters in the Jesus story, those who came to witness his birth. The writer succeeds in explaining the paradoxes of birth and death as they are developed in the poem. Her approach is a simple but effective one.

8. WRITING ABOUT A POPULAR SONG LYRIC: PERSONAL RESPONSE AS EVALUATION

Silence

Often—and it is becoming a pretty regular thing these days—when I become depressed and tired of the silence of people I step out into the darkness of night to relax and think. I can take people only for so long, and then I want to scream. I find myself asking: "What in the hell is going on here?" I get tired of the usual escapes: drugs, drinking, or talking to my parents or a priest. After a while these human escapes from humanity put me right back where I started. I sometimes find consolation in just being aware of the situation Man is in, but after trying to get action and finding only the silence—it brings me down pretty fast. I'm not sure whether it is better to live with questions unanswered or with answers to questions that no one cares to ask. So I take a walk in the darkness of the night, trying to understand how some people can feel satisfied.

There are several forms of silence: the silence of people who are unaware; the silence of people who are aware; and the silence of those who won't allow themselves the self-education that is required to become aware of the faults that are in need of correction. From "The Sound of Silence" by Paul Simon, I receive the impression that he was trying to break through the silence of aware people—people who talk day after day without saying or hearing a thing; fools who are creating a guiding system of life which is not to be questioned, just accepted as it is now until the end of time. But time is running out for such silence. Today more than ever the silence is being shattered—but time may still run out.

I feel very strongly about the plight of the American Indian and Negro. It makes me very sad to see so many satisfied people walking around, when there is so little to be satisfied with today. I know life cannot really be described in words, but I feel that whatever it is it is an individual thing. By living every day of our lives honestly, trying to seek out the corruption that must be corrected and to find love instead of quick, unjust hate, perhaps we can manage to create a satisfactory environment for ourselves and each other.

Comment   The student's essay reveals a thorough understanding of the song lyrics, even though it does not deal directly with the verses. What is written in the first paragraph parallels the experience narrated in the poem, but it is the student's own. The second paragraph paraphrases several of the ideas in the third stanza of the song. The details of the third paragraph grow out of the previous one and take the reader back to the sense of discontent expressed at the beginning of the essay. The ending reflects the spirit of the original lyrics, although the student expresses a stronger sense of hope and idealism than the composer.

The student's response to the song—being able to express a parallel experience and similar thoughts—comments on the validity of the poem. This is a private, nonformal kind of evaluation, but it is meaningful because one knows that the student has been involved with the verses.

9. WRITING ABOUT A BOOK OF THE BIBLE: A CREATIVE ADAPTATION

The Prisoner

Joseph Brennin had never been in jail before now. This environment was completely strange to him. In fact, it was so strange that he was unable at first to formulate any opinion as to whether or not he even minded the situation he found himself in. Perhaps it was the total shock of being dumped into such a radically different setting than the one he had known that caused Joe to be so overwhelmed. Joe had been fairly well off and respected in his province. He owned a large ranch with many great vineyards and orchards. His house had been simple, but not without a few luxuries, and he had a wife whom he loved, as well as four children —three boys and a girl. But now, all of his past life seemed greatly remote. The cell he lived in was simple. His bed consisted of a mat on some wood planks about three feet off the ground. A pipe that stuck through one of the walls was constantly dribbling water. It had a valve attached to it that increased the water's flow a little, but could never be shut completely off.

Joe had been taken to the jail only four days ago. He had been traveling to the southern end of the province by himself where he planned to meet a friend who had recently purchased land there. Joe was arrested by the provincial police quite suddenly one day, and when he asked them what he was charged with, he was answered with arrogant silence. All he was told was that his trial was forthcoming and that he would not be allowed to meet with his lawyer before then. His valuables were taken into custody, and he was put into the cell with three others named Eli, Bill, and Zo.

It was at this time, four days after Joe's arrest, that the officials of the prison were discussing what was to become of Joe.

"You mean he was arrested for no reason at all?" asked the older officer.

"None. None that I can find anyway. I assume that it was just a case of the jitters that caused the police to arrest him. He is a respectable man, but strange to this part of the province."

"No reason at all, eh?" The older officer smiled ironically at this. "What have times come to?"

"Well," said the younger officer, "what shall we do with him? Is he to be released?"

"No, not yet. We'll wait for the governor. He's due here next week, and there's a chance that Mr. Brennin's arrest has something to do with that. The governor will know what to do with him, and in the meantime we can conduct our own investigations."

"But what if he isn't guilty of anything? We will be injuring an innocent man."

"Everyone is guilty of something," said the older officer. "He has been arrested and if we should begin punishing him, he will be certain that we are aware of some wrong he has committed. Just wait and see. I'll bet you five dollars that sooner or later he'll confess to something."

"All right. It's a bet."

It was late into the hot afternoon when Joe was led back to his cell. He was exhausted from the day's work which had consisted of pulling a cart filled with rocks along a track. His shoes had been taken away from him leaving him barefoot to work on the hot gravel. Twice that day he had fainted from exhaustion. When this happened, he was taken into the shade and revived, only to be sent back to his work. Now both his hands and feet were blistered and bleeding. Joe's movements were stiff and slow when he entered the cell. He went straight to his bed and collapsed.

"Boy oh boy! They sure did you over good," said Eli.

Joe sat staring for several moments, then said, "I wish I had never set foot in this lousy country. I wish my parents had never brought me to life within this country's borders. I would like nothing better than to see this province burned off the face of the earth and its name erased from any map ever made of it. I wish that all memory of this country, of its history, of its existence, of its ideals would be thoroughly obliterated. It's not enough for me that this hell pit should be demolished. How could this happen? How could it be that a man like me who has kept to himself, who has served his friends, who has been fair with his employees, who has always faithfully paid his taxes should be treated like this by his own government? This is completely unreasonable. It's outrageous. I am in every way a worthy citizen. I have done nothing that could injure this country or any of its people, but still I am tortured like this. I am treated like filth when my intentions are all good. What kind of a government is it we have that allows this to happen to a person like me?"

"The government is hard but it isn't stupid," said Eli. "It watches out for those who support it and lets them share in some of the spoils. That's the way it always works. If you're the 'good citizen' you say you are, then you don't have anything to worry about. There'll be someone looking out for you."

"But I'm telling you the truth," said Joe. "I've done nothing wrong and yet I'm treated like this." Joe raised his bloody hands to emphasize his point. "This is the case, and it leaves me with an uneasy feeling. Now I begin to see my country, our government, for what it is. My imprisonment was a stupid blunder, no doubt an error caused by some bureaucrat who has never even heard of me before. The government doesn't even know its people, much less serve them. The government is a big dumb beast, completely uncompassionate and moving by means of its own inertia only."

At this last statement, Bill was suddenly aroused. He turned to Zo and said, "Did you hear that, pal? Joe here thinks he was just thrown in this cell for nothing." Both he and Zo laughed at this. "Let me tell you something, friend," Bill said to Joe, "you don't get thrown in here just for doing nothing. Now we're all here for something that we did, and we know it. I'm sure you've done something wrong even though it may be small or you wouldn't be here. You're just not willing to admit it. If you were such an upright citizen, you'd certainly be getting your rewards now."

"That was a pretty dumb thing to say," said Joe. He was bitter now. "I know for myself that I am innocent, and if you decide not to believe me, I guess I can't blame you because you have no way of knowing. If you do believe me, it will have to be on faith, for I tell you I'm guilty of nothing. But as for your assumption that everyone is thrown in here for some reason, let me ask you this: if this government of ours is so efficient, so responsive as to pick out every minor threat to either itself or to its people, why is it that we don't have a society free from crime? Why is it that criminal acts are so commonplace in our province, and that no one even gives them a second thought? Surely any crime I may have committed unwittingly could not deserve as much punishment as this, while thieves and murderers run around loose. Wouldn't it be much simpler to conclude that the government's actions are sporadic, with no plan or central thrust?"

Zo was next to speak. "The kind of government that you speak of is almost frightening. If all that you say is true, then what we have is no government at all. All that could be said to exist is some force, and that would be quite frightening if we were to assume that it had no direction, for even if it were directed towards evil, we would have some way of predicting its actions. As you put it, however, we could never reason what will happen next. But on close examination, I think you'll find that our culture is a living and breathing one. Look, for example, at our institutions. This prison is an instance. If our government was so cold and irrational, would it make sense to have jails rather than just killing off social undesirables, which would probably make more sense? No. There is an ideology implied here, and though I may not agree with it, it is nevertheless there. Jails are made to deter crime, the idea being that a person will think twice before facing the possibility of going to jail. Take your trial. Your best bet would be to plead guilty, but during your plea break down into weeping as you confess not only guilt for your crime but for everything you've ever done and eventually for even your very existence. Throw yourself on the mercy of the court and say you've repented and they'll just lap it all up."

Joe sat quietly smiling at Zo for a moment. Then he said quietly, "Just the same, I admit to being guilty of nothing. If the government had an ideology, if I have been sent here with the idea that I could eventually be of some use to society, then how could this same government that looks so closely after my welfare be so blind to the facts of any crime I may have committed? I don't see any kind of reason working here. I can't find any explanation that would support an understanding of how the machinery of this country works. The only thing I can say is that this country seems to be moving on an insane course to nowhere. The only thing I can understand is that this pain is inflicted on me for apparently no reason. I understand the pain, but I don't understand the reason for it. Every time I think I have found the reason, I turn and it's not there. I have lived and worked within this country, and yet I can't even understand how my government functions and what all my work has amounted to. All I want is for someone to answer me."

• • •

It was 4:30 in the afternoon when the governor arrived at the prison. He spoke only briefly with the prison officers before he asked to be led down to Joe's cell.

"You are quite lucky, Mr. Brennin," said the older officer. "The governor himself is here in town to personally see to your release."

"That's right," said the governor. "This isn't a joke. You're free to leave now."

Joe stood silently staring at the governor while the cell door was opened and Joe was led out. Finally he said, "Well, I'm certainly happy that this thing is over, but let me say that I sure think you do a lousy job of running things in this province. Why was I locked up like this? Don't your police have any respect for good people such as myself?"

"Good people such as yourself, eh?" said the governor. "I don't know who the hell you think you are, but I'll tell you this. The functioning of our government is greatly more important than any one person's individual needs could ever be. The government is run for the benefit of all the people and must serve all of the people as best it possibly can. The needs of all the people are so much more important than yours alone that I don't feel any need to apologize to you whatsoever, although I may be able to recognize that you have been dealt with unjustly. But that is beside the point. It is inconceivable to me that you should question the workings of our government, for to assume that we should do anything wrong would be to assume that our government is working to undermine itself, which would be ridiculous. Besides, it seems to me that you're being rather vain to place yourself in the role of critic of your government. Look at how vast and great our government is. In what position are you to judge the institutions upheld by our government, or the economy our government controls? How would you grade our foreign trade and relations? Would you design your own laws by which to rule the nation? Or would you like to show me how I should do my job?"

"I'm sorry," said Joe. "I admit I was wrong for doubting my government, and I see now that I have a lot yet to learn before I may question it."

And so, Joseph Brennin was released from prison, given back his valuables, and left to visit his friend before returning to his home and family. However, before Joe left the prison, he was given a large sum of money by the governor to compensate for the time Joe had spent in jail.

Comment Anyone familiar with the Book of Job—sometimes called a story, sometimes a drama, sometimes a symposium—will know that the parallels between this adaptation and the original are extremely close, even down to details of the dialogue. The story could have been written only after a careful study of the original and a thoughtful reconsideration of it. What is particularly effective is the way the secular version ends with the same perplexity and irony as the Book of Job itself. If the ending of this modern version seems abrupt and unsatisfactory, it merely comments on the original. The student did not invent the ending; he merely found a parallel that gives us a clearer perspective of the things that happen to Job. The story works constantly in two directions: backward to the original and forward to the implications for our future.

This particular story is a fine example of writing about literature by creating literature, not using the original merely as a point of departure, but showing the implications and revealing how an ancient work can comment on the current scene.

Individuals as Their Own Models

These nine examples of writing—all done by college students, mostly freshmen—indicate different degrees of excellence, of literary sophistication, of detachment and involvement, and reveal varying interests in the effects of literature. They indicate that writing about literature is within the capability of any thoughtful person. What they by all means should suggest is that there is no stereotype for the theme about literature. In fact, prescribing any kind of model would defeat the main theme of this book: the idea that you yourself have to come to some realization about the world of literature and its effects on you. Given some understanding of the elements that go to make up literature, you have to find the best way you possibly can to make clear your own understandings and feelings. In fact, in the process of writing about literature, you may find that you have come to know yourself in a more meaningful way.

Glossary of Additional Literary and Rhetorical Terms

For terms not included here, consult the general index.

Absurdity   A philosophical mode of thought whose fundamental premise is that man's condition and actions are necessarily absurd in a purposeless and irrational world. The literature embodying this attitude characteristically demonstrates the absurdity of existence in grotesque but paradoxically meaningful—often meaningless—ways. In Edward Albee's *The Sandbox,* a sandbox on stage serves as a grave for Grandma, who is unceremoniously dumped into it by Mommy and Daddy. In Eugene Ionesco's *The Bald Soprano,* Mr. and Mrs. Martin, man and wife, engage in an inane dialogue as if they do not know one another (see pp. 74–75), while a clock, according to the stage directions, must strike "so loud that it makes the audience jump." Joseph Heller's *Catch-22* portrays the mad, mad antics of Yossarian and those around him who grasp for survival and sanity in a war-torn world. Of the numerous works of absurdist literature by these and other twentieth-century writers like Harold Pinter, Jean Genêt, Jean-Paul Sartre, Anthony Burgess, and Kurt Vonnegut, the one work that has already established itself as a classic of the post-World War II era and represents a prototype of absurdism is Samuel Beckett's

Waiting for Godot. One critic has aptly phrased its essential statement: "I wait, therefore I am—maybe."

In subjects and techniques, plays and novels in this mode exploit the bizarre, the fantastic, the symbolical, and the experimental, often using cinematic devices. In words and actions, they are comic, even hilarious; in intent and effect, they may be despairing and tragic. *See* **Existentialism** and **Expressionism.**

Affective fallacy   A phrase implying that the tendency to judge the merit of a work by its emotional effect on the reader is misleading. If such a standard were applied, sentimental works might consistently be rated superior.

Alliteration   *See* **Sound effects.**

Anacolouthon   A rhetorical device by which a writer accidentally or deliberately breaks off his line of thought and then begins again. The strategy may be used intentionally to suggest hesitation, to insinuate, or to create a dramatic effect:

> The opposition must be—whatever we do, we must do it decisively and quickly.

Anaphora   A rhetorical figure in which one or more words are repeated at the beginning of successive sentences or lines of poetry. A similar repetition at the end is called epistrophe.

> Where the city of the faithfulest friends stands,
> Where the city of the cleanliness of the sexes stands,
> Where the city of the healthiest fathers stands,
> Where the city of the best-bodied mothers stands,
> There the great city stands.
> > —Walt Whitman, "Song of the Broad-Axe"

When the two devices are combined, as in the Whitman poem, the figure is called symploche.

Antistrophe   *See* **Ode.**

Apostrophe   A rhetorical trope (q.v.) in which the writer turns away from his subject to address directly an object, abstraction, or person, usually dead or absent. The shift is both emotional and dignified, therefore most appropriate in serious and stately contexts:

> So when this corruptible shall have put on incorruption, and this mortal shall have put on immortality, then shall be brought to pass the saying that is written, Death is swallowed up in victory.
> O death, where is thy sting? O grave, where is thy victory?
> > —I Cor. 15 :54–55

Assonance   *See* **Sound effects.**

Asyndeton A rhetorical figure which omits conjunctions between a series of words, phrases, or clauses:

I am alone, I am lost, I am abandoned.

The opposite figure of deliberately including conjunctions for a special stylistic effect is called polysyndeton:

> Then Job arose, and rent his mantle, and shaved his head, and fell down upon the ground, and worshipped, and said; Naked came I out of my mother's womb, and naked shall I return thither: the Lord gave, and the Lord hath taken away; blessed be the name of the Lord.
> —Job 1:20–21

Augustan Originally a reference to the remarkable literary age of Horace, Ovid, and Vergil under the Roman emperor Augustus (27 B.C.–A.D. 14). English writers in the first half of the eighteenth century appropriated the label for their own period because they considered the political stability of Augustus' reign a model for English government and sought to recapture the symmetry, precision, and decorous bearing of the Latin poetry of that same age. The term is used to name neoclassical resurgences in the literature of other nations, most notably France's *le grand siècle* of Corneille and Racine. *See* **Classicism.**

Ballad Originally a folk form with its roots in oral tradition, the ballad is distinguished by a simple stanzaic pattern readily chanted or sung (*see* **Ballad stanza**), often with a refrain. A ballad characteristically tells a story, using abrupt transitions, terse dialogue, and supernatural elements. Its themes are traditional ones—love failed, escape from danger, a great feat. The oldest English ballads date from the thirteenth to the fifteenth centuries. "Broadside ballads" in the eighteenth century gave up traditional folk themes but exploited the ballad's popularity with a mass audience by indulging in satire. The ballad's tie with folk literature loosened even more as its treatment became more literary and personal in examples such as Coleridge's *The Rime of the Ancient Mariner* and Ezra Pound's "The Ballad of the Goodly Frere."

Ballade A poem consisting of three stanzas and an envoy, with the last line of the first stanza recurring as a refrain at the end of each of the other stanzas and the envoy. The stanzas may vary from eight to ten lines in length, but the eight-line rime royal is commonly used. The envoy is usually half the length of the stanzas and in substance dedicated to a person or personification. The form is French in origin and popular in medieval poetry. Chaucer wrote a "Ballade of Good Counsel"; Swinburne's "A

Ballad of Dreamland" is an eight-line ballade. The form continues to be popular today.

Ballad opera   A development in eighteenth-century England as a reaction among English authors and critics to the invasion of the English theater by Italian opera. The most successful of these satiric song-dramas was John Gay's *The Beggar's Opera* (1728), which often travesties the artificiality and excesses of the Italian style.

Ballad stanza   A four-line stanza with alternating tetrameter and trimeter lines. The rhyme scheme is ordinarily *abcb*, with the shorter lines rhyming. Other ballads, however, use different rhyme schemes. Coleridge's *The Rime of the Ancient Mariner* is written in ballad stanzas.

Baroque   A literary style which attempts to achieve with words what artists of the baroque manner accomplished in painting, sculpture, and architecture. In art, the style is marked by a restlessness, dynamism, emotionalism, and ornateness. In literature, the style is characterized by sensuous appeal, metrical dissonance, paradoxes, extravagant conceits, and asymmetricality. The manner is represented by Luis de Góngora in Spain, Giambattista Marino in Italy, and the Metaphysical poets, particularly Richard Crashaw, in England.

Bathos   From the Greek word meaning "depth," perhaps best defined by Alexander Pope in the subtitle to his mock treatise *On Bathos* as "the art of sinking in poetry." Bathos is frequently an unintentional effect of "sinking" when a poet's Pegasus forgets how to fly. The effect is therefore either humorous or pedestrian or both. Even the best poets are capable of bathetic effects, as in Wordsworth's poem "Simon Lee":

> Few months of life has he in store
> As he to you will tell,
> For still, the more he works, the more
> Do his weak ankles swell.

Belles-lettres   Translated, the French term means "fine letters." It is used by the French to describe the serious pursuit of literary studies. As appropriated to English usage, however, its connotations of nice elegance and genteel quality have emphasized the subjective, sometimes precious, quality of individual taste; and the term and its adjective form "belletristic" have assumed a pejorative cast. The words are therefore used to describe writing that may be polished but thin in substance or those persons whose appreciation of literature is wholly idiosyncratic and whimsical rather than analytical and studied.

Bildungsroman   A term borrowed from the German, meaning literally "a novel of education." A *bildungsroman* is typically a novel in which a young man grows and matures and comes to some realization about life and himself. Goethe's *Wilhelm Meister's Apprenticeship* is an early example; Dickens' *David Copperfield* and Maugham's *Of Human Bondage* are later ones.

Bombast   A form of pretentious, overly inflated diction intended for a grandiose effect, but resulting often in general windiness. Bombast is therefore at times used intentionally for comic effect, as in a speech by Pistol in Shakespeare's *Henry IV, Part II:*

Shall dunghill curs confront the Helicons?
And shall good news be baffled?
Then Pistol lay thy head in Furies' lap.

Bucolic   *See* **Pastoral.**

Burlesque   A literary technique which mocks persons, acts, or a particular kind of style by exaggerating, demeaning, or otherwise distorting the manner. When a trivial subject is treated in an elevated manner, like Pope's mock epic "The Rape of the Lock," the result is "high burlesque." When a serious subject is trivialized, like the judgment of the dead in Byron's "The Vision of Judgment," the result is "low burlesque."

Parody differs from burlesque in that it is based on a particular work, using words and structures from the original to reduce it to absurdity. Joyce Kilmer's "Trees" has been frequently parodied. Burlesques satirize a general manner, as Cervantes' *Don Quixote* is in part a burlesque of the chivalric tradition as recorded in the medieval romances.

Caesura   *See* **Versification.**

Caricature   A device of deliberate distortion by taking the most obtrusive traits of a person or fictional character and exaggerating them. The strategy is common in satiric cartoons, but it is equally common in literature as a means of making particular characters absurd or simply as a means of heightening their identity, as Dickens often does with his characters.

Carpe diem   A phrase from Horace meaning "seize the day," used to describe a motif in poetry which emphasizes living for the pleasure of the moment, for tomorrow may never arrive. Robert Herrick's poem "To the Virgins To Make Much of Time," which

begins with the line "Gather ye rose-buds while ye may," epito-
mizes the theme.

Catharsis   Originally a Greek medical term meaning a purga-
tion, especially of the bowels. In the *Poetics*, Aristotle uses the term
metaphorically to describe how pity and fear are diminished by the
effects of tragedy. Whether he meant that the purging of pity
and fear occurs in the viewer, who leaves the theater with a sense
of release from having vicariously experienced the suffering of a
worthy hero, or whether the purging is a trait of the tragic plot
itself, in which the hero learns to see himself more deeply, has
been a source of continued debate.

Chaucerian stanza   *See* **Rime royal.**

Cinquain   An American version of the Japanese haiku, consisting of five lines of varying length. The first line must be two
syllables, followed by lines of four, six, eight, and two syllables,
respectively.

Classicism   An attitude or frame of mind that holds that the
established, orderly principles of conduct epitomized by Greek and
Roman traditions are superior to the anti-traditionalism and emotional spontaneity associated with romantic habits of mind (*see*
Romanticism). Although the distinction between classical and
romantic attitudes is never firm, classicism in literature is generally taken to imply rational control, traditional thinking, and
decorous restraint in style as opposed to private insight and the
liberated spirit.

In the seventeenth and eighteenth centuries throughout Western Europe, a large number of writers deliberately looked back
to ancient models, attempting to restore authority, discipline,
and clarity to literature. The impulse, whenever it surfaces, is
known as neoclassicism.

Prominent among the writers of neoclassical temperament were
Corneille, Racine, and Molière in France; Dryden, Swift, Pope,
Addison, and Johnson in England; and Benjamin Franklin in
America.

Comedy   Like tragedy, comedy is a way of viewing life; it is not
exclusively a literary term. Essentially, it is a way of looking at
life that invites tolerance for the follies and weaknesses of men.
If tragedy tends to elevate man, showing us the strength of
man in his capacity to endure the trials of life, causing us to
look up to him, comedy changes the perspective. We are not looking up at figures larger than life or identifying with them on an
equal level. Comedy tends to place characters in such roles that the

audience views detachedly, or the audience is able to assume a superior stance that causes it to make observations on the action; it is led to comment, criticize, and find amusement in the follies of everyday affairs.

Comedy lacks the inevitableness of tragedy. Man is not trapped. In comedy, characters are permitted to emerge from complex situations and continue on their way in good spirits. It is a part of poetic justice and the spirit of comedy that offenders of good sense, good humor, and proportion will be punished. Living must go on. Even though comedy is an antidote to tragedy, it does not ignore the sadness of life, but it does show man's capacity to jump back from the edge of disaster, to cope with living. It is a positive view.

The outside world itself tends to be the arena of comedy, not the universe or the inner being. It often deals with everyday affairs, with nonheroic characters, with manners in the broad sense of the word, with the absurd and petty nature of man, with foibles, with the playful side of serious subjects like love, ambition, and corruption. Because comedy is a detached view, it can even make disaster funny. The hijinks of farce would be only calamities if we identified with the victims and felt that they were being seriously injured. Comedy does not permit a preoccupation with grief.

Comedy is didactic in a number of ways. Its view of life may be instructive to those who see only gloom and catastrophe in human affairs. Its tendency to highlight incongruity can sensitize viewers to the humor of situations; its frankness provides an antidote to self-deception. Its pronouncements about vice and folly may be forthrightly moral. Its wit may be a corrective. All in all, it is a glorification of man's love of living, despite the problems and adversities of everyday affairs.

Literary history includes a number of different labels identifying comedies with particular themes and conventions: romantic comedy, *commedia dell'arte*, comedy of humours, comedy of manners, sentimental comedy, and tragicomedy. But these can be meaningfully explained only in terms of the times during which they thrive and in terms of specific conventions that differentiate them. See separate entries for each.

Comedy of humours Plays in which characters are shaped to illustrate one of the prevailing humours of medieval physiology. The predominance of one kind of liquid in the body, either blood, phlegm, yellow bile, or black bile, was supposed to produce a corresponding sanguine, phlegmatic, choleric, or melancholic disposition in the person. A play like Ben Jonson's *Every Man in His*

Humour (1598) utilizes the device freely, but other comedies include characters, like Jacques in *As You Like It*, who owe their eccentricity to a particular humour. Even a serious character like the melancholic Hamlet may be viewed as a humour character.

Comedy of manners Basically a sophisticated kind of comedy concerned with social manners in the broad sense of the term. The characters are usually drawn from high society; the dialogue is witty; the satire sharp. William Congreve's *The Way of the World* (1700) is often cited as a prototype. The form was popular in Restoration England and eighteenth-century France, but Oscar Wilde and Bernard Shaw gave the type new vigor in modern times.

Commedia dell'arte A highly stylized form of comedy originating in Italy in the sixteenth century and popularized throughout Europe by traveling companies. The actors of the company improvised the dialogue consistent with the outline of a plot and appropriate to the stock characters, some of whom wore masks. The most familiar figures were a foolish merchant Pantalone; a pompous and pedantic man of learning called the Doctor; a boastful but cowardly captain Scaramuccia; the youthful Arlecchino or Harlequin, famous for his tight, multicolored costume; Pulcinella, a long-nosed buffoon (later the Punch of Punch and Judy puppet shows); Columbine, the sweetheart of Harlequin; and Pierrot and Pierrette, clown lovers. These same characters are still commonly seen in the circus, ballet, opera, and painting and are often made into dolls, puppets, and marionettes.

Common measure *See* **Hymn stanza.**

Conceit A word derived from "conceive," which originally described an image or comparison, but which is now almost exclusively associated with exaggerated, far-fetched metaphors, commonly found in poems written in the Petrarchan or Metaphysical manner. In Elegy XIX, John Donne addresses his mistress:

> My mine of precious stones, my empery,
> How blest am I in this discovering thee!

In a humorous twist on the traditional inflated praise of the mistress in the Petrarchan manner, Shakespeare wrote:

> My mistress' eyes are nothing like the sun;
> Coral is far more red than her lips' red;
> If snow be white, why then her breasts are dun;
> If hairs be wires, black wires grow on her head.

The Metaphysical conceit is also common in the twentieth century among poets who have found new values in seventeenth-century poetry:

> Dear love, these fingers that had known your touch,
> And tied our separate forces first together,
> Were ten poor idiot fingers not worth much,
> Ten frozen parsnips hanging in the weather.
> —John Crowe Ransom, "Winter Remembered"

Consonance   *See* **Sound effects.**

Counterpoint   *See* **Versification.**

Couplet   Two rhyming lines, usually of the same meter. Couplets are called end-stopped if each line is a complete grammatical unit:

> Those oft are stratagems which errors seem,
> Nor is it Homer nods, but we that dream.
> —Alexander Pope, *An Essay on Criticism*

Run-on couplets are those in which the sense of one line is carried over to the next. The blending of two lines is called enjambment:

> Whan Zephirus eek with his swete breeth
> Inspirèd hath in every holt and heeth
> The tendre croppes, and the yonge sonne
> Hath in the Ram his halve cours y-ronne,
> —Chaucer, "Prologue," *The Canterbury Tales*

Courtly love   A literary tradition of love-making that flourished in the Middle Ages and continued to find expression in various forms throughout the Renaissance. The concepts of courtly love grew out of the socio-economic conditions that prevailed in feudal times. The first and most important principle of the courtly tradition was that love and marriage were irreconcilable because desire as a matter of free choice could not exist in a relationship in which duty and necessity were the compelling factors. Secrecy was an essential condition of beginning love; fear was a stimulus. Lyrics in which poet-lovers express their adulation for remote and cold mistresses and their own frustration at their inaccessibility were actually disguises for adulterous and illicit relations, although at times a lover expresses his desire for a requited love quite unambiguously. Love is an art concerned with vows, oaths, and complaints. The lover weeps, sighs, sorrows, and dies; the mistress refuses to love or is inconstant. The outward expression of love was formal, polished, and elegant.

This art of love first became a system in the north of France. The themes were crystallized in the narrative poems of Chrétien de Troyes and set down as a code in *The Art of Courtly Love* (1170) by Andreas Capellanus. By the middle of the twelfth century, the tradition had become a mock religion. It might have died with the decline of the troubadour in the thirteenth century if it had not been given new inspiration and refinement by poets like Guinicelli, Cavalcanti, Dante, and Petrarch. *See* **Petrarchanism** and **Neo-Platonic love.**

Decorum   Attention to propriety and appropriateness, a notion most popular in periods marked by a classical belief in right order and "everything in its place." The term is used generally to suggest a code of behavior based on tastefulness and restraint. Its literary use more specifically applies to the suitability of language to the thought of a particular work. Dryden explained decorum as "appropriateness of words to action"; Jonathan Swift wrote, "Proper words in proper places makes the true definition of style."

Dénouement   A French term meaning "an untying," referring to that part of a novel, story, or play in which the complications of the plot are unraveled or in which the characters come to some realization about themselves. Dénouement is therefore the culmination of the action following the rising action and climax.

Deus ex machina   Literally meaning "God out of a machine." The term originally had reference to the act of lowering a character to the stage by means of a machine to represent the intervention of some supernatural being in the affairs of men. By extension, *deus ex machina* refers to any sudden appearance, miraculous event, or improbable device which extricates characters from dilemmas.

Doggerel   A term used to describe uninspired and inferior verse. Sometimes used deliberately for comic effect by distorting meters and rhyme, as in Samuel Butler's mock-heroic poem *Hudibras:*

> Besides, he was a shrewd philosopher,
> And had read every text and gloss over;
> Whate'er the crabbed'st author hath,
> He understood b' implicit faith,

Dramatic monologue   A form of dramatic poetry in which one character's spoken lines and, at times, his private thoughts are set down as a means of self-characterization. The poem also includes an awareness of setting and other characters to whom words may be spoken. Robert Browning's "My Last Duchess" is perhaps the single most famous poem of this type, although

Edgar Lee Masters and Edwin Arlington Robinson among American poets have produced equally fine character portraits.

Eclogue *See* **Pastoral.**

Elegy In Greek and Roman poetry, the elegy was not bound by a particular subject matter but by an exclusive use of the elegiac couplet. Love was a predominant theme. In the Augustan age, the elegy reflected the cosmopolitan spirit of a sophisticated age, treating the lighter aspects of contemporary life and a love *à la mode*. In English poetry, the convention of a prescribed meter was abandoned. Even though love elegies continued to be written by poets like Marlowe and Donne in imitation of Ovid, Catullus, and Propertius, the form since the time of the Renaissance has become almost exclusively associated with a poem written upon the death of a particular person. Among noteworthy examples are Milton's "Lycidas," Shelley's *Adonais*, and Arnold's "Thyrsis," all written in the pastoral manner; Tennyson's *In Memoriam*, an extended series of lyrics written over a period of seventeen years in memory of Arthur Henry Hallam, has been called the greatest elegy of the nineteenth century.

Enjambment *See* **Couplet.**

Epanalepsis A rhetorical figure which produces an echo effect by repeating the beginning word at the end of the sentence:

When wilt thou save the people? O God of mercy, when?

—Josiah Booth

Epic A long narrative poem consisting of numerous episodes and adventures, drawn together by a central heroic figure and the poet's own purpose. Epics frequently represent a glorification of a race or nation, although poems like Milton's *Paradise Lost* or Dante's *The Divine Comedy* may treat the ultimate destiny of all mankind. Milton states that his theme is to "assert Eternal Providence,/And justify the ways of God to men."

Because of the themes of high importance and the grand scale of epics, the style is characteristically elevated and dignified. Homer's *Iliad* and *Odyssey* became the models for all subsequent literary epics of the Western world, although the conventions that grow out of them were more and more formalized by the tradition. Thus the stylization of later epics can be best understood in terms of earlier examples. Epics characteristically begin with an invocation to a muse for inspiration and the recital of a question and answer, which often set the theme of the epic. The action then follows a set formula. It begins in the middle of things (*in medias res*), followed by a section during which the hero narrates antecedent events (retrospective narration); the major action then continues to the end. In the course of the narration, the epic usually includes descriptions of battles and tests of strength, catalogs of characters or ships or arms, a visit to the underworld, the intervention of the gods to protect the hero, and long debates about actions to be taken. The description is frequently interspersed with extended comparisons, usually referred to as epic similes.

Among the great literary epics in this tradition are Vergil's *Aeneid,* Tasso's *Jerusalem Delivered,* Spenser's *The Faerie Queene,* and Milton's *Paradise Lost.* Among the so-called folk epics, probably written without knowledge of the literary tradition described above but reflecting the same spirit of an heroic age, are the Anglo Saxon *Beowulf,* the French *Song of Roland,* the Finnish *Kalevala,* and the German *Nibelungenlied.*

Epigram   Now a pithy statement, in prose or verse, marked by humor and wit, often turning on a twist of thought or play on words. The form, originally an epitaph in the Greek, later developed into a short polished poem on almost any topic. In Latin literature, it was cultivated by Martial; in English literature, it is particularly associated with Donne, Jonson, and Pope. The two-line epigram is particularly common:

> Thy flattering picture, Phryne, is like thee
> Only in this, that you both painted be.
>
> —John Donne, "Phryne"

Epilogue   The counterpart of the prologue (q.v.) at the ending of a play, in which one of the actors usually remains on the stage to reflect upon the action, to philosophize or moralize, and to send the audience on its way. Shakespeare's *As You Like It* ends in this fashion.

Epistrophe   *See* **Anaphora.**

Epithalamion, also **epithalamium**   A wedding song, a kind of occasional poem, usually of lyric beauty, popular when it was customary to escort the bride and bridegroom to the wedding chamber. The poem is therefore a song in honor of the couple, including praise of them, a description of the wedding and the wedding feast, and blessings upon their future. Examples may be found among the works of the classical poets, including Pindar, Theocritus, and Catullus; among English poets, Sidney, Donne, Jonson, and Herrick may be included. Perhaps the most celebrated poem of this kind is Edmund Spenser's "Epithalamion," written on the occasion of his own wedding to Elizabeth Boyle (1594).

Epode *See* **Ode.**

Existentialism A philosophical mode of thought whose starting point is that we can know things only as they are, not as they are in essence. This position is summarized in the familiar expression: "Existence precedes essence." Existentialism therefore operates in a human setting; it depends upon human consciousness as its means of perception. It is concerned with the actual, the human, and the possible. It offers no guarantees of success or ultimate salvation, as science and traditional religion tend to do. It urges the individual to act, because he *is* what he makes of himself. Man defines himself.

The diversity of thinkers who are labeled existentialists, both atheists and religious theologians, can be explained mainly by the fact that existentialism, in its preoccupation with the human situation, focuses mainly upon the analysis of possibilities open to man in his relation to other men and conditions. It therefore embraces many positions and attitudes. In 1947, Jean-Paul Sartre asserted that existentialism was positive and optimistic, not negative and despairing. As a philosophy, of course, it can be either.

In the post-World War II period, in the aftermath of mass destruction and killing, existentialism became associated with all that was painful, dreadful, hopeless, and unstable about the human condition. Existentialism seemed to explain the desperate situation in which man found himself. The spiritual climate of post-World War II Europe did not create existentialism; it illustrated the negativism implicit in it and set the tone of the movement for decades to follow. Existentialism became faddish as an expression of the meaninglessness and absurdity of life. Its themes found expression in literature and art; its anti-authoritarianism led to protest against established values and institutions, even to mannerisms of dress which reflected individual contempt for bourgeois respectability.

In philosophy, the movement is associated with Karl Jaspers, Martin Heidegger, Søren Kierkegaard, and Jean-Paul Sartre. In literature, its spirit is reflected in the works of Sartre, Simone de Beauvoir, Albert Camus, and André Malraux.

Expressionism A literary movement with its origins in Germany in the pre-World War I period, but strongly influencing later writers, particularly dramatists. Expressionism converted the skepticism and malaise of the *fin-de-siècle* writers into an aggressive activism, directed against bourgeois values, industrial materialism, and social injustice. At the same time that writers realistically appraised the conditions of life around them, they assumed a messianic role, calling for a regeneration of all human values, a new purity and serenity in men, and a return to the values of primitive Christianity. Prominent among expressionist dramatists were Georg Kaiser, Ernst Toller, and Fritz von Unruh.

The lasting influence of expressionism, however, was its effect on structure, stagecraft, and acting in the drama. In order to express their ideas fully, expressionist dramatists, using Strindberg as their model, abandoned the illusionism of the realistic stage and exploited any theatrical device which would convey both idea and feeling. Thus lighting, music, stylized acting, and distorted scenery gained new emphasis; the apron stage and revolving stage facilitated a different kind of action made up mainly of short scenes. These techniques have continued to be developed in the drama of the second half of the twentieth century. Even though expressionism is closely associated with drama, the fiction of Franz Kafka and James Joyce employs techniques that can be called expressionistic.

Fable A story told for a specific moral or allegorical purpose, commonly represented in literature by the beast fable, which uses animals acting and speaking like human beings. In essence, the fable instructs about human affairs, but depends on the power of the writer to keep the reader simultaneously aware of animal traits and human tendencies. The fables of Aesop and LaFontaine are successful in this way. More extended and sophisticated uses of the beast fable for satiric purposes include Chaucer's *Nun's Priest's Tale,* Spenser's *Mother Hubberds Tale,* John Dryden's *The Hind and the Panther,* and George Orwell's *Animal Farm.*

Fabliau A short tale, in verse or prose, usually bawdy and humorous in its details, particularly associated with the Middle Ages, although parallel examples may be found in early Latin and Oriental literature. The emphasis in these stories is on practical jokes and lively action, although considerable interest also arises from the satire directed toward the clergy, marriage, and hypocrisy. Chaucer gives fabliaux to the Miller and the Reeve in *The Canterbury Tales.* Others are included in Boccaccio's *Decameron.*

Figure A covering term used to refer to any kind of metaphorical, symbolical, or rhetorical variation of ordinary words and speech patterns. *See* **Trope.**

Folio An old bibliographical term used to designate the size of a book. Folio refers to a sheet of paper folded once to make two leaves or four pages; quarto is a sheet folded twice to make four leaves or eight pages; and octavo is a sheet folded three times to make eight leaves or sixteen pages. The First Folio of Shakespeare's plays (1623) therefore refers to the format in which they appeared. Many of the plays also appeared originally in quarto editions.

Fin de siècle A French term meaning "end of the century," now signifying a general spirit of decadence, but more specifically referring to the "art for art's sake" movement at the end of the nineteenth century associated with the work of Walter Pater, Oscar Wilde, and Aubrey Beardsley. Their interest in aesthetics, polish, and refinement contrasted sharply with the strong bourgeois values of the age, suggesting an idea of effeteness and elitism among the exponents of the movement.

Free verse Free verse is free only in the sense that it abandons the rules of traditional prosody. It is often a verse that sets up its own rhythmic patterns based on a principle of cadences rather than regular accents. Lines of free verse might be thought to fall into arcs rather than feet, suggesting the effect of a musical phrase. Two lines of Whitman's "Out of the Cradle Endlessly Rocking" show the wavelike surging and ebbing of his verse:

From your memories sad brother,

from the fitful risings and fallings I heard;

From under that yellow half-moon late-risen and swollen as if with tears.

Each of the arcs has from two to four major stresses; these key words are pulses, but they do not come at regular intervals. They are determined by the sense of the line and the rhetorical devices the poet chooses to use. Free verse depends strongly on repetition, parallelism, recurring images, and sound effects other than rhyme. The lines may vary in length, often determined by the sense, the rhythmic arcs, the emphasis, and rhetorical devices such as anaphora. Stanzas are flexible in form like those of the ode. Free verse accommodates itself to natural speech patterns, to the logic of the writer's thoughts, and to his desire to evolve the shape of his own poem. It need not be expansive, as it often is in poems by Whitman and D. H. Lawrence. It can also convey concise, tight thoughts, as it does in poems by Wallace Stevens, William Carlos Williams, and E. E. Cummings.

A strong precedent for free verse in English comes from Hebrew poetry, particularly as it is translated in the King James version of the Bible. Passages from Job, Isaiah, Song of Solomon, and particularly the Psalms illustrate the dependence of this verse on principles of symmetry:

> I am come into my garden, my sister, my spouse:
> I have gathered my myrrh with my spice;
> I have eaten my honeycomb with my honey;
> I have drunk my wine with my milk:
> Eat, O friends; drink, yea drink abundantly, O beloved.
>
> —Song of Solomon, 5:1

The principles of free verse are also inherent in Old English poetry. The lines are irregular in length, with stresses falling on the words demanded by the sense. Each line consists of two halves divided by a well-defined caesura, with two stresses in each half and an unspecified number of unstressed syllables. The two parts are joined by the alliteration of two or three of the stressed syllables:

> Oft Scýld Scéfing   scéaþena þréatum,
> mónegum mægþum   méodo-sètla oftéah
>
> —*Beowulf*

Despite these requirements, the lines are flexible and clearly rhythmical in the spirit of free verse.

One other variety of the free metrical line is called sprung rhythm, invented by Gerard Manley Hopkins. Its most marked feature is the juxtaposition of stressed syllables without intervening unstressed ones. It is therefore sometimes called an accent meter. A line of sprung rhythm is measured by the number of strong accents, not the number of feet or syllables. Like Old English verse, with which it shares common principles, sprung rhythm also depends heavily on alliteration and other sound effects:

> I caught this morning morning's minion, kingdom of daylight's dauphin,
> dapple-dawn-drawn Falcon, in his riding
>
> —Gerard Manley Hopkins, "The Windhover"

Unlike other free verse poets, Hopkins frequently wrote in traditional stanza forms and used rhyme.

Gothic novel A form of horror story which arose in the eighteenth century as an early manifestation of the romantic spirit. Gothic was descriptive of the pervasive gloomy atmosphere and grotesquerie suggested by medieval cathedrals. Novels and ro-

mances written in the manner featured an abundance of villain-
ous characters, sensational events, secret passageways and dun-
geons, macabre effects, and supernatural happenings. The prototype
of the Gothic novel was Horace Walpole's *Castle of Otranto* (1764),
although the best known one is probably *Frankenstein* (1817) by
Mary Wollstonecraft Shelley. Modern writers continue to elaborate
on the basic type.

Haiku   A Japanese form, consisting of three lines designed to
give a sharp image. The lines consist of five, seven, and five
syllables, respectively.

Hamartia   *See* **Tragic flaw.**

Heroic drama   A kind of grandiose drama popular in England
after the opening of the theaters in 1660 following the Puritan
interregnum. The plays emphasized themes of honor and love,
featuring heroes of noble valor and heroines of unexceptional
purity. The plots were involved and marked by stirring scenes
of action and violence, inflated speeches, and triumph of the
hero in war and love. John Dryden's *The Conquest of Granada
by the Spaniards* (1670) represents the type; it is mocked by
George Villiers in his play *The Rehearsal* (1671).

Horatian ode   *See* **Ode.**

Hubris or **Hybris**   *See* **Tragic flaw.**

Humanism   An intellectual movement throughout Europe in
the fourteenth, fifteenth, and sixteenth centuries, marking a shift
in emphasis from a preoccupation with metaphysical issues and
otherworldliness in the Middle Ages to a new concern with man
and his problems in this life. The change in intellectual climate
identifies the beginnings of the Renaissance with its glorification of human potentiality, the importance of the individual, and
the spirit of inquiry and discovery. One of the important manifestations of Humanism was its revival of ancient classics in
order to seek out models for human conduct and thinking in the
ancient writers. New emphasis was placed on learning the original
languages (Erasmus taught Greek at Cambridge), and transla-
tions of early works were made available in England for the first
time. Among the distinguished English Humanists and scholars
were William Grocyn, Sir Thomas More, Thomas Linacre, John
Colet, and William Lyly.

Hymn stanza or **Common measure**   A four-line stanza with
alternating lines of iambic tetrameter and iambic trimeter, rhym-

ing *abab* or *abcb*. The hymn stanza is similar to the ballad stanza but much more strictly measured.

Idyll *See* **Pastoral.**

Imagism A literary movement in poetry during the first quarter of the twentieth century, strongly influenced by the ideals of literary impressionism—the experience as seen and felt by the poet, but phrased in sharp, concentrated visual images, like one from Ezra Pound's "Dance Figure":

White as an almond are thy shoulders;
As new almonds stripped from the husk.

The aims of the movement were set down in the preface to an anthology entitled *Some Imagist Poets* (1915). The basic principles were (1) to use exact words from common speech rather than decorative ones; (2) to avoid echoing old rhythms as a way of finding new ways of expression; (3) to place no limits on the subject matter of poetry; (4) to write in precise images; (5) to avoid the "blurred and indefinite" in favor of the "hard and clear"; (6) to assert the belief that "concentration is of the very essence of poetry."

Besides Pound, the leader of the movement, and Amy Lowell, one of its chief advocates, Imagist poets included Hilda Doolittle, John Gould Fletcher, Richard Aldington, T. E. Hulme, F. S. Flint, and D. H. Lawrence. Even though these poets soon abandoned the purely imagistic poem because of its narrow range of expression, the movement was to influence twentieth-century poetry strongly in its move toward freer rhythms and more inclusive subject matter.

Impressionism Less well defined as a literary movement than as an art movement, but associated with the principle that the artist considers the way he feels about characters and scenes more significant artistically than facts about them. Impressionism therefore emphasizes a highly personal view of art, in which the writer's own temperament, experiences, and moods predominate. In German literature, the movement included the plays of Arthur Schnitzler and Hugo von Hofmannsthal and the early fiction of Thomas Mann, often reflecting a bittersweet skepticism and a general *fin-de-siècle* atmosphere. Impressionism marked a transition from the realistic and naturalistic emphasis of the nineteenth century to a neoromantic, symbolic tradition of the twentieth century. *See* **Expressionism** and **Imagism.**

Intentional fallacy A critical phrase implying that the success of a literary work need not be judged in terms of the author's own design or intentions concerning it. They might be unknown or extremely limited. The work can be viewed as an object in itself.

Interlude *See* **Morality play.**

Invocation A formal address to the deity, a muse, or to some other source of inspiration for the poet. The invocation traditionally marks the beginning of an epic, but many other poems, like Shelley's "Ode to the West Wind," begin in a similar way:

O wild West Wind, thou breath of Autumn's being,

. . .

Wild Spirit, which art moving everywhere;
Destroyer and preserver; hear, oh, hear!

Kenning A type of abbreviated metaphor particularly characteristic of Old English poetry. Kennings tend to be circumlocutions; they describe persons or things in a picturesque way: "heath-stalker" for stag, "whale-road" for ocean, and "jewel of the heavens" for the sun.

Limerick A catchy five-line stanza, rhyming *aabba*. The third and fourth lines are shorter than lines one, two, and five.

Litotes A rhetorical term for understatement that gains its particular effect by phrasing in the negative what it wishes to say positively. "This is no small accomplishment" means "This is an accomplishment of considerable magnitude"; or "That is not at all unpleasant" means "It is pleasant."

Lyric Originally, a poem to be sung by an individual to the accompaniment of the lyre and differentiated in Greek times from choric odes. Although lyrics are no longer written necessarily to be sung, they do remain the expression of feeling by a single voice, whether the poet's own or that of a persona. The lyric is unspecified in form or theme, although it is usually a brief poem. Poems that are narrative, dramatic, or discursive tend to be classified differently and are referred to as lyrics only if the verse is sufficiently moving and musical to justify the epithet "lyrical."

Malapropism A term used to describe the kind of humorous blundering with language typical of Mrs. Malaprop in Sheridan's play *The Rivals* (1775). A malapropism ordinarily confuses two words resembling one another in sound: *supercilious knowledge* for *superficial knowledge; psychosemantic illness* for *psychosomatic illness; prostrate gland* for *prostate gland.*

Masque A highly stylized form of dramatic entertainment, particularly popular in the sixteenth and seventeenth centuries. Masques, usually commissioned for a special celebration, were performed both indoors and outdoors on the estates of wealthy nobles. Masques were often performed only once because they were written for a particular person or occasion. The host and members of his family frequently were given parts. The productions were lavish, including elaborate costumes, singing, dancing, and pageantry, at times involving machinery which allowed the spectacular effect of supernatural figures entering "from above" (*deus ex machina*). The plots were thin, but highly moral in tone, often casting mythological and allegorical characters in key roles. The poetry was lyrical. One of the popular features of the entertainment was the anti-masque or antic-masque, which featured animals or men in animal disguise and usually represented a counterforce, like the deadly sins, to the good characters of the main plot. The names of Ben Jonson and Inigo Jones are intimately associated with the period during which the masque flourished.

Melodrama Melodrama bears a close relation to tragedy in that it concerns itself with the calamities and afflictions of human experience, but it does so with a different effect. Melodrama appeals to the passions and sympathies of an audience without necessarily producing the catharsis associated with tragedy. Melodrama tends to be less complex than tragedy; it views the issues of life as clearly right and wrong, not as ambiguous and paradoxical as tragedy views them. It emphasizes plot and situation rather than depth of character. The tendency of melodrama to make clear-cut distinctions has made it a suitable literary form for presenting political and moral problems. In serious melodrama, virtue does not always win; in popular melodrama, of course, virtue always triumphs.

The implications of the word *melodramatic* are those drawn from melodramas concerned with sensational effects, exciting action, and flamboyant characters. It suggests extravagance and intrigue. Yet one need not associate all melodrama with plays like *Uncle Tom's Cabin* and *Ten Nights in a Bar-room,* designed for their propaganda value and famous for their stock characters and elements of suspense. The term might also usefully describe many Renaissance and Jacobean plays, which exploit intrigue and shock, yet whose characters fall short of tragic suffering and realization.

Metaphysical conceit *See* **Conceit.**

Meter *See* **Versification.**

Miracle play   A form of medieval religious drama popular in the fourteenth and fifteenth centuries. The term *mystery play* is sometimes used to designate those plays based exclusively on Biblical material as opposed to the *miracle play*, concerned with the lives of saints and the conversion of pagan characters. Only a very few plays of the second variety are extant. More commonly, however, *miracle play* is used to include the far more numerous plays based on scripture.

The miracle plays were at first performed in the church, then in the churchyard, and finally were divorced altogether from the church when the responsibility for their staging and cost was assumed by the town guilds. The guilds often vied with one another in the elaborateness and ingenuity of the staging. Two types of performances were common: the stationary, in which the platforms were built in the town square and the audience moved from one to another to view a different play; and the processional, in which the audience remained stationary and the plays were mounted on wagons and rotated among the assembled groups. Miracle plays were often called Corpus Christi plays because the Thursday following the eighth Sunday after Easter was the main occasion for the performance of entire cycles of plays.

Four cycles of miracle plays are extant in English and one in Cornish: the Chester cycle, consisting of 25 plays; the York cycle, consisting of 48 plays; the Coventry cycle, consisting of 42 plays, and the Wakefield cycle, consisting of 32 plays and including *The Second Shepherds' Play*, perhaps the best known of these dramas. The Cornish cycle consists of 50 episodes divided into three main parts. All of these plays draw on Biblical themes extending from the story of Creation to the Day of Judgment. It has been estimated that they cover eighty-nine different episodes from the Bible.

Despite the religious nature of the plays and their design to instruct and to bolster the faith of the laity, the plays were not without their humor. Among the early humorous characters were the devil himself, Noah's wife, depicted as a nag and husband-beater, and Herod, a raving tyrant, whose ranting behavior became the norm for the expression "to out-herod Herod." Cycle plays continued to be produced well into the sixteenth century. They represent a strong, continuous tradition of dramatic production from the Middle Ages to the Renaissance that prepared England for the full flowering of its drama during the Age of Elizabeth.

Morality play   A later development of the medieval play, abandoning scriptural characters and stories as the basis for action and substituting allegorical characters and personifications. The plays were written to enforce a moral, sometimes ethical in nature, sometimes doctrinal, and sometimes political. One of the best examples is the *Castle of Perseverance* (1471), in which the central figure representing all mankind is attacked by the seven deadly sins, defended by the cardinal virtues, and forced to take refuge in the Castle of Perseverance. In the final judgment scene, his many sins are forgiven him and he is saved by Christ's mercy. An equally famous morality play is *Everyman* (ca. 1500), which still enjoys performances today.

The weightiness of these allegorical dramas was balanced by the introduction of humorous characters, particularly the devil and Vice, whose amusing scenes together added variety and anticipated the kind of brief humorous interlude which became popular in the fifteenth century.

Mystery play *See* **Miracle play.**

Naturalism Naturalism is sometimes differentiated from realism in time and in degree. It was a continuation of the realistic view into the late nineteenth and twentieth centuries; it was also an intensification of that view. Emile Zola was the progenitor of the school, although he preferred to call it a method. Zola maintained that literature would have to apply the methods of science to the understanding of human nature and behavior. Thus, ideal naturalism would be a kind of clinical reporting; men would be natural organisms under observation. Naturalism did not put limits on subject matter; the German naturalistic dramatist Gerhart Hauptmann was labeled "the painter of the putrid."

Besides its detached objectivity and harsh realism, naturalism emphasized a deterministic view of life, based on the natural laws of heredity and environment. The tendency to see man as a victim of a purposeless universe and vast social and economic forces working against him leads to a prevailing mood of pessimism in naturalistic works.

Besides Zola and Hauptmann, naturalistic writers include Georg Büchner, a forerunner of the movement in Germany; Stephen Crane, Frank Norris, and Jack London in America.

Neoclassicism *See* **Classicism.**

Neo-Platonic love New impetus was given to the fashionableness of Petrarchanism in the sixteenth century by Pietro Bembo and his followers, who combined Platonism with this popular tradition. The doctrines of Platonism coincided admirably with the Petrarchan conventions and in many instances served as a philosophical commentary on a previously unexplained love. As Marsilio Ficino interpreted Platonic love, the souls of true lovers departed from heaven under the same astral influence; true love in this world was merely a recognition of like soul quality and the fusion of those souls. Passion emanated from the soul, not the senses. Love itself was contemplative in nature. The lover's praise of his mistress' beauty was not a cataloging of her physical charms but, refined from sensuousness, an expression of the idea of woman. This kind of love ennobled the lover and moved him to excel in virtue in order to be deserving of his mistress. With its emphasis on love as a matter of mind and soul, Neo-Platonism moved the literary expression of love to a higher plane of thought but often left the lyrics themselves highly formal and empty of feeling.

Neoromantic *See* **Romanticism.**

Novella A term borrowed from the Italian, originally used to designate short narratives in prose, like those in Boccaccio's *Decameron,* popular during the Middle Ages and Renaissance. Since the development of the short story in the nineteenth century, novella has been used to designate a story of approximately 30,000 or 40,000 words, between the typical length of the short story and the minimum length of the novel of approximately 60,000 words. The intermediate length of the novella permits the writer to achieve effects different from either the short story or the novel, so that the difference is not strictly one of length. Conrad's *Heart of Darkness,* Faulkner's *The Bear,* and Hemingway's *The Old Man and the Sea* may be cited as examples.

Objective correlative A means of objectifying and expressing emotion by finding a set of equivalent circumstances or objects which will evoke the same feeling as the one the writer wishes to express. Thus, T. S. Eliot illustrates, the state of Lady Macbeth's mind during the sleepwalking scene is conveyed by a series of sensory impressions.

Octavo *See* **Folio.**

Ode A stanza of an unspecified number of lines and rhyme scheme, given to the praise of a person or a particular subject, such as Emerson's "Ode: Inscribed to W. H. Channing" or Keats's "Ode on Melancholy." Two traditions exist, the Pindaric and the Horatian.

The Pindaric ode follows the pattern of odes composed by Pindar for choral recitation. The form consists of three stanzas called the strophe, antistrophe, and epode. Strophe means "turn" and refers to the movement of the chorus as it chanted the ode up one side of the orchestra; the antistrophe was the second stanza as the chorus moved down the other side. The epode was the final stationary song, sometimes called the stand, as the chorus faced the audience.

The Horatian ode, in imitation of the poems of Horace, is an ode in which subsequent stanzas of the poem follow the pattern of the first stanza, like Keats's "To a Nightingale." An irregular ode is one like Wordsworth's "Ode on Intimations of Immortality" or Coleridge's "Ode on Dejection" in which the stanzas vary both in length and pattern.

Onomatopoeia *See* **Sound effects.**

Oration At the present time, any formal speech, but in ancient times an address which followed a prescribed form set down by Quintilian and embodied in the orations of Demosthenes and Cicero. Traditionally, the oration had seven parts, although some of them were at times varied or combined: (1) exordium, introducing the subject; (2) narration, presentation of the circumstances and background of the issue; (3) proposition, a brief statement of the point to be established; (4) division, a definition of terms and an outline of the parts; (5) confirmation and proof, the main part of the speech including the arguments; (6) refutation, the anticipation of objections; and (7) peroration, a summarization and final impassioned plea. Milton's *Areopagitica* (1644) is a notable example of the classical oration in English.

Ottava rima A stanza consisting of eight lines of iambic pentameter, rhyming *abababcc*, used by Byron in *Don Juan* and "The Vision of Judgment."

Oxymoron A rhetorical trope (q.v.) that links together two sharply contrasting terms. Instances are particularly common in poetry: "darkness visible" (Milton); "living deaths, dear wounds, fair storms, and freezing fires" (Sidney); "By this good wicked spirit, sweet angel devil" (Drayton); "Let the rich wine within the goblet boil,/Cold as a bubbling well" (Keats).

Parody *See* **Burlesque.**

Pastoral A tradition of literary expression using the rural life of shepherds and shepherdesses as the model for a kind of idyllic existence. The term *bucolic*, derived from the Greek word meaning "herdsman" or "rustic," designates the same tradition. Pastoral poems were frequently written as eclogues, taking the form of a dialogue between two shepherds.

Pastoral poetry has its origins in the poems of Theocritus, a Greek poet of the third century B.C., whose idylls, as they were called, depicted simple scenes of life in Sicily. To a Roman citizen like Vergil, pastoral life was a contrast to the complexities of cosmopolitan life and an ideal escape. It also became a convenient way of commenting indirectly on a corrupt society and thus a suitable vehicle for satire and allegory (Vergil's *Fourth Eclogue* was long interpreted as a pagan anticipation of the birth of Jesus). As a sophisticated literary mode, pastoralism was popular among English writers of the Renaissance, including Sidney, Spenser, Shakespeare, Milton, and Marvell.

Pathetic fallacy   A phrase used by John Ruskin in *Modern Painters* to describe the tendency of poets to ascribe human attributes to inanimate objects, particularly to manifestations of nature. Although Ruskin disapproved of what he considered the untruth of phrases like "cruel, crawling foam" and "the spendthrift crocus," the phrase is now used in a neutral sense to characterize the poetic illusion that objects of nature feel and react as men do. Compare **Personification.**

Pathos   From a Greek word meaning "suffering," often a part of tragedy but not synonymous with true tragedy. Pathos is an effect produced by literature and other art forms which arouse feelings of pity and compassion and often grow out of scenes of misfortune, misery, death, or separation. Pathos appeals directly to the feelings. The difference between pathos and sentimentality is at times only one of degree.

Personification or **prosopopoeia**   A rhetorical and poetic way of describing abstractions or inanimate objects in human terms. Personification is common in poetry, as in lines by Sir Philip Sidney:

But words came halting forth, wanting Invention's stay;
Invention, Nature's child, fled step-dame Study's blows.

Petrarchanism   The Italian poet Petrarch (1304–1374) was to exercise a major influence on the love lyric because he was accepted by later Renaissance writers as their master. Their model was his poetry to Laura in the *Canzoniere*, expressing his unattainable but ennobling love over a period of twenty-one years for a married woman who scholars now believe may not have existed at all. Petrarch's poetry embodied not only an idealistic concept of chaste devotion but also an essentially human passion. His imitators at least presumed to follow these ideals and the elegance of his style, but hit mainly on the eccentricities of his verses—the antitheses, the puns, the conceits, and the exaggerations. These devices became the marks of the Petrarchan manner, which in the fifteenth and sixteenth centuries moved more and more toward extravagance.

Pindaric ode   *See* **Ode.**

Polysyndeton   *See* **Asyndeton.**

Prologue   In drama, a brief introductory statement by one of the actors, sometimes designated as the Chorus, to set the action, to summarize the theme of the play, or to offer the author's apologies or comments. The Prologue to *Romeo and Juliet* may be accepted as fairly typical. *See* **Epilogue.**

Prosody   *See* **Versification.**

Prosopopoeia   *See* **Personification.**

Purple passage   A familiar phrase used in criticism to designate a particularly quotable passage, especially if it is characterized by elaborateness, eloquence, or colorfulness. The phrase was first used by Horace in *The Art of Poetry* when he described "one or two purple patches . . . sewed on to make a fine display in the distance." The phrase is frequently used in a pejorative sense to describe a passage that seems to strive too hard for its effect.

Quarto   *See* **Folio.**

Quatrain   A flexible stanza of four lines, sometimes of equal length and sometimes not (*see* **Ballad stanza** and **Hymn stanza**), with rhyme schemes of considerable variety. The heroic quatrain or elegiac quatrain consists of lines of iambic pentameter, rhyming *abab*. Blake uses it in "The Little Black Boy" and "The Chimney Sweep." The four-line stanza used by Fitzgerald in *The Rubaiyat of Omar Khayyam* is iambic pentameter, rhyming *aaba*. The quatrain of Tennyson's *In Memoriam* is iambic tetrameter, rhyming *abba*. Frost uses tetrameter lines rhyming *aaba* in "Stopping by Woods on a Snowy Evening," but the final stanza is *aaaa*. The quatrain is a highly flexible and popular form among English and American poets.

Realism   A way of looking at life and writing about it without illusion or without an imaginative transformation of the facts, recording what is with as much objectivity as the writer is capable of assuming. A realistic view also tends to take a certain focus: it is more likely to be preoccupied with the middle class rather than the nobility, with hardship rather than ease, with commonplaces rather than extravagances, with humanitarian values rather than aesthetic ones, with materialism rather than idealism, with the ordinary and everyday rather than the exotic and unique. By its selection of details it tries to be representative of the whole of daily living.

Realism, of course, has prevailed in all literature at all periods. On occasion, however, usually in reaction to the excesses of a previous age, it serves as a substantial bread-and-butter diet for the literary artist. Modern realism had its roots in the movement that began in France in the 1830s with the efforts of Honoré de Balzac to set down a complete picture of the social life of contemporary France in a monumental project entitled *The Human Comedy.* In twenty years, Balzac produced more than 95 novels, novelettes, and short stories in an effort to complete his depiction of contemporary manners. By midcentury, realism had taken hold through the added efforts of Gustav Flaubert and the brothers Goncourt and was being denounced as immoral and ugly. But the movement was to move to further extremes of verisimilitude in the work of Guy de Maupassant and Emile Zola. *See* **Naturalism.**

Associated with realism in English literature to varying degrees were Daniel Defoe, sometimes referred to as the father of English realism, Henry Fielding, George Eliot, William Makepeace Thackeray, Anthony Trollope, and Thomas Hardy. American realists include William Dean Howells, Mark Twain, Henry James, Theodore Dreiser, and Sinclair Lewis. The Russian scene of the nineteenth century was particularly conducive to the realistic temperament and produced two of the world's greatest realists, Tolstoy and Dostoevsky.

Refrain   *See* **Sound effects.**

Repetition   *See* **Sound effects.**

Rhyme   *See* **Sound effects.**

Rime royal or **Chaucerian stanza**   A stanza consisting of seven lines of iambic pentameter, rhyming *ababbcc,* so named because James I of Scotland wrote a poem in this form. Chaucer uses it in *Troilus and Criseyde* and other poems.

Romance   From a Latin adverb *romanice,* meaning "in the Latin manner," used to refer to early French dialects, later specifically to Old French, and finally to anything written in French. Languages derived from Latin are commonly referred to as Romance languages.

Today, romance suggests a love story. The emphasis probably derives from those medieval romances which involve some of the most famous lovers of all times—Tristan and Iseult, Launcelot and Guinevere, Aucassin and Nicolette, and Floris and Blanchefleur. Although a love interest was often included in the romances, it was not an indispensable ingredient. The basic material was knightly activity. The romance may therefore be defined as a story of adventure, often based on historical characters but narrating fictitious incidents, frequently involving the miraculous and supernatural, written in verse or prose. The earlier romances dating from as early as the twelfth century are in verse; the later ones extending through the fourteenth century tend to be in prose. Romances are frequently classified under three headings, indicating the source of their materials: the matter of Greece and Rome, stories about Troilus and Criseyde, Aeneas, and Alexander; the matter of France, stories about Charlemagne and his knights; the matter of England, stories about Arthur and the familiar Knights of the Round Table.

Although the romance as a story of adventure shares elements with the epic, the romance tends to be a more superficial form, less concerned with character development, organic unity, and lofty purpose. The romance, however, does reflect a chivalric age and is a source of information about social status, mores, and interests during the Middle Ages.

Romantic comedy A term that refers specifically to Renaissance comedies about lovers in an idyllic, pastoral, or woodland setting, rather than to any comedy about love. The comedy depends strongly on disguised characters and the intrigue and laughter that grow out of the deception. Shakespeare's *As You Like It* is one of the best examples.

Romanticism A spirit or attitude that prevails at any period when the claims of the individual, his feelings, and his freedom to act and respond without the restraints of the past are given first priority. Romanticism as a manifestation of literature is almost always a part of a cycle, a breaking away from the established traditions of a previous age that honors moderation, restraint, and decorum. The great Romantic era of Western literature occurred in Europe and America during the nineteenth century, following the period of Neoclassicism in the seventeenth and eighteenth centuries. In Germany, the chief exponents were Goethe, Heine, and Schiller; in France, Dumas, de Musset, Hugo, and George Sand; in Russia, Pushkin and Lermontov; in England, Wordsworth, Coleridge, Keats, Byron, Shelley, and Sir Walter Scott; in America, Poe, Emerson, Thoreau, and Whitman. In Germany and England, the movement was early (Goethe and

Scott died in 1832); in France and America, the movement was delayed.

Because Romanticism typically represents a regeneration of individual values, it is difficult to generalize about its particular manifestations. Among individual writers, however, the nineteenth-century movement marked a new interest in the freedom of the common man, a concern for natural genius, intuition, spontaneity, and sensation, a belief in nature as a source of inspiration and goodness, a preoccupation with the mystical, exotic, and supernatural, a revival of interest in the Middle Ages, popular ballads, and ancient folk legends, a glorification of the natural and primitive as opposed to the ordered and civilized, a distaste for imitation, rules, and elegance, a disapproval of traditional forms and artifices, and a special trust in the powers of the imagination. Romanticism was a literary expression of the spirit of revolution that had already occurred in the political life of France and the American colonies.

Any period that marks a revival of those qualities which are peculiarly Romantic is usually referred to as a period of Neoromanticism. The abstract and symbolic plays of William Butler Yeats may be considered neoromantic.

Scansion *See* **Versification.**

Sentimental comedy A development in comic drama during the eighteenth century as a reaction to the indecency of comedies of manners during the Restoration period. The emphasis of these plays falls on characters who confess their faults, repent their erring ways, and thus demonstrate the perfectibility of human nature. Excessive feelings, pathetic scenes, and moral sentiments abound, although the plays are not without satiric purpose. Sir Richard Steele's four comedies, including *The Conscious Lovers* (1722), represent the type.

Sentimentality An exploitation of the tender feelings in such a way that the reader reacts negatively to the oversensitizing. Sentimentality is consistently used as a term condemning a surfeit of sweetness, an excess of tenderness, an overdisplay of gentleness, or a melodrama of tears. Recognition of sentimentality is, of course, relative. Some readers like to indulge their feelings; others are far more protective of their soft spots.

Sermon In medieval times, the form of the sermon often followed the model of the classical oration. It fell into six parts: (1) theme, the announcement of the text and translation of it into the vernacular; (2) pro-theme, an expression of humility on the part of the preacher and an invocation for God's help; (3) dilation, an expansion on the text; (4) exemplum, an illustration in the form of a story drawn from life or literature; (5) peroration, the application of the lesson; and (6) a closing epilogue, usually in Latin.

Seven cardinal virtues   *See* **Seven deadly sins.**

Seven deadly sins   According to medieval theology, the cardinal sins were pride, envy, wrath, sloth, avarice, gluttony, and lust. These were considered "deadly" because they were punished by spiritual death unless the offender underwent true penitence. The sins are widely referred to and personified throughout the literature of the Middle Ages and Renaissance. The corresponding seven cardinal virtues were faith, hope, and love (the Christian virtues) and prudence, justice, fortitude, and temperance (the temporal virtues derived from Plato).

Simile   A particular kind of comparison, marked by the use of the words *like* or *as:*

> Yet in these thoughts myself almost despising,
> Haply I think on thee, and then my state,
> Like to the lark at break of day arising
> From sullen earth, sings hymns at heaven's gate.
> —Shakespeare, "Sonnet 29"

The term metaphor is often used to include the simile.

Sonnet   See pp. 61–63.

Sound effects   One of the chief delights of poetry is its sound, sometimes its melodiousness, sometimes its suggestion of actual sounds, sometimes the appropriateness of sound to meaning. Word choice is, of course, the most important factor in the creation of sound in a poem, but the choices themselves are often determined by devices that poets use. Seven of these are a part of the poet's repertory of techniques.

Alliteration

Sometimes referred to as beginning rhyme and limited as a principle to the repetition of beginning consonant sounds, although hidden alliteration often occurs in internal and end syllables. In lines like the following from Shakespeare's "Sonnet 30," both the alliteration of *s*'s and *w*'s and the repetition of the *s* in medial and final positions are working together to produce the total sound effect:

When to the sessions of sweet silent thought
I summon up remembrance of things past,
I sigh the lack of many a thing I sought,
And with old woes new wail my dear time's waste.

Alliteration has operated as a major poetic technique in English poetry from Anglo-Saxon times to the present.

Assonance

Repetition of vowel sounds throughout a poem, either exact duplications or resemblances. The device is frequently used to establish a tone appropriate to the thought of the line. Compare the opening lines of Milton's companion pieces on joy and melancholy:

Hence loathéd melancholy
  Of Cerberus and blackest midnight born
In Stygian cave forlorn
  'Mongst horrid shapes, and shrieks, and sights unholy!

—"L'Allegro"

Hence vain deluding joys,
  The brood of folly without father bred!
How little you bestead,
  Or fill the fixéd mind with all your toys!

—"Il Penseroso"

Melancholy is described in rounded, back vowels, low-pitched in sound; joy is described in opened, front vowels, high-pitched in sound.

Assonance can also be used as a variation on exact rhyme when a word falls in a final stressed position, as in lines from Dylan Thomas' "And Death Shall Have No Dominion":

And death shall have no dominion.
Dead men naked they shall be one
With the man in the wind and the west moon;
When their bones are picked clean and the clean bones gone,

Consonance

A kind of half-rhyme or consonantal rhyme in which the consonants are parallel but the vowels are different. Wilfred Owen uses consonance instead of exact rhyme in "Arms and the Boy":

Let the boy try along this bayonet-blade
How cold steel is, and keen with hunger of blood;
Blue with all malice, like a madman's flash;
And thinly drawn with famishing for flesh.

Consonance is sometimes used synonymously with alliteration or as a term to describe the recurrence of consonant sounds at the end of words.

Onomatopoeia

An attempt to reinforce the meaning by using words that suggest the sounds they describe. The device can be used imitatively, as in Kipling's "The Song of the Banjo":

> With my *"Tumpa-tumpa-tum-pa tump!"*

Or it can be used suggestively with varying degrees of subtlety:

> Over the cobbles he clattered and clashed in the dark inn-yard,
> And he tapped with his whip on the shutters, but all was
>   locked and barred.
> > —Alfred Noyes, "The Highwayman"

> The ice was all around:
> It cracked and growled, and reared and howled.
> > —Coleridge, *The Rime of the Ancient Mariner*

> The curfew tolls the knell of parting day,
> The lowing herd winds slowly o'er the lea,
> > —Thomas Gray, "Elegy Written in a Country Churchyard"

> The lark, that tirra-lirra chants,
>   With hey! with hey! the thrush and the jay,
> > —Shakespeare, *The Winter's Tale*

Repetition

The repetition of single words is a common technique and done almost always with a dramatic effect:

> Blow, bugle, blow, set the wild echoes flying,
> And answer, echoes, answer dying, dying, dying.
> > —Tennyson, *The Princess*

> We're foot–slog–slog–slog-sloggin' over Africa—
> Foot–foot–foot–foot–sloggin' over Africa—
> (Boots–boots–boots–boots–movin' up an' down again!)
>   There's no discharge in the war!
> > —Kipling, "Boots"

> Lisp'd to me the low and delicious word death,
> And again death, death, death, death,
> > —Whitman, "Out of the Cradle Endlessly Rocking"

Refrain

Repetition of a complete line at the end of a stanza, often with a musical effect or an intensification of the meaning of the words. It is commonly used in French stanza forms like the ballade and villanelle. Henley's "Ballade of Dead Actors" repeats the line "Into the night go one and all" at the end of each of three stanzas and the envoy.

Rhyme

The identity of two words with one another because of the resemblance of their sounds. If the repetition of sounds is close, like *eyes* and *sighs,* the rhyme is said to be exact or perfect. But many rhymes are suggestive rather than exact, like John Crowe Ransom's rhyme of *drunkard* and *conquered* or C. Day Lewis' *womb* and *home* or Emily Dickinson's rhyme of *shown* and *cocoon.* These are sometimes referred to as half-rhymes, slant rhymes, off-rhymes, or various other terms which suggest their approximate nature. *See also* **Consonance** and **Assonance.**

The most familiar rhyme, of course, is that which occurs at the end of a line in a stressed syllable, called end-rhyme. Other rhyme, however, may occur internally, tending to divide a long line into two definite parts if it occurs at the caesura, as in Poe's well-known line from "The Raven":

Once upon a midnight dreary, while I pondered, weak and weary.

Rhymes like *dreary* and *weary,* with the stressed syllable followed by an unstressed one, are called feminine rhymes. Rhymes of single stressed syllables are masculine. Rhymes are designated as double (*bolder, shoulder*) or triple (*intuition, erudition*) in terms of the number of rhyming syllables. Some rhymes appear to be only eye-rhymes, like Marvell's

And yonder all before us lie
Deserts of vast eternity.

Although some modern writers use eye-rhymes intentionally, their presence in earlier poems often testifies to changes in pronunciation that have taken place. In fact, rhymes are one of the important sources of knowledge concerning the pronunciation of sounds in the past.

Rhyme can be used as a source of humor by matching unexpected words, as in Gilbert's lyrics for *The Mikado.* The rhyme for *exist* turns out to be *philanthropist.* One of Ogden Nash's favorite devices for humor was to force words into a pattern of rhyme:

One kind of sin is called a sin of commission, and that
        is very important,
And it is what you are doing when you are doing something
        you ortant.
                —"Portrait of the Artist as a Prematurely Old Man"

Functionally, the use of rhyme goes beyond its sound qualities.

Its occurrence interlocks the parts of a poem, it gives emphasis, it reinforces the meaning, it establishes the tone of a poem. In these ways, it operates as one of the poet's most effective resources.

Spenserian stanza   A nine-line stanza, eight lines of which are iambic pentameter and the final line a hexameter. The rhyme scheme is *ababbcbcc*. It is, of course, the stanza form of Spenser's *The Faerie Queene*, but other poets have used it also in major works—Byron in *Childe Harold*, Shelley in *Adonais*, and Keats in "The Eve of St. Agnes."

Stanza   A grouping of lines of verse in a particular pattern. The stanza may sometimes coincide with a complete sentence; at other times, it is comparable to a paragraph representing the longer development of an idea. A stanza may be a logical unit, or it may be a strictly formal unit defined in terms of line length, meter, and rhyme scheme. *See* **Versification.**

Separate entries on stanza forms include:

Ballade	**Ottava rima**
Ballad stanza	**Quatrain**
Cinquain	**Rime royal**
Couplet	**Sonnet**
Haiku	**Spenserian stanza**
Hymn stanza	**Tail-rime stanza**
Limerick	**Tercet**
Ode	**Villanelle**

Stream of consciousness   A narrative technique by which the writer attempts to reproduce the timeless flow and free association of the inner thoughts of a character. The disconnectedness, irrelevance, lack of structure, and uncensored thoughts are successful in revealing the subconscious mind and allowing a psychological probing not possible by traditional narrative devices. Molly Bloom's interior monologue at the end of James Joyce's *Ulysses*, transcribed without any punctuation, is one of the most sustained uses of the technique in literature.

Strophe   *See* **Ode.**

Stylistics   Sometimes used interchangeably with *style*, but more specifically refers to the application of linguistics to the study of style. Stylistics is therefore primarily descriptive, placing emphasis on measurable, quantitative data, for example, word frequency, average sentence length, characteristic use of grammatical forms, and transformations.

Symploche   *See* **Anaphora.**

Synaesthesia A special metaphorical effect in which one of the senses is used to describe the perception of another sense:

But the creaking empty light
Will never harden into sight . . .

—Edith Sitwell

Tail-rime stanza A six-line stanza in which longer lines, usually tetrameter couplets, are alternated with a shorter line, called "the tail," usually a trimeter. The rhyme scheme is *aabccb*. Many variants of the stanza occur, however, chief among which is Robert Burns's use of the tail-rime in various familiar poems like "To a Mountain Daisy," "To a Mouse," and "To a Louse." His form is three tetrameters, followed by a two-foot "tail," another tetrameter, and a final "tail." The rhyme scheme is *aaabab*.

Tenor and **Vehicle** Useful critical terms from I. A. Richards' *The Philosophy of Rhetoric* for discussing metaphor. The vehicle refers to the figure of speech itself, the tenor to the underlying idea. The metaphor embraces both. The opening lines of Milton's "Lycidas" will serve as an example:

Yet once more, O ye laurels, and once more,
Ye myrtles brown, with ivy never sere,
I come to pluck your berries harsh and crude,
And with forced fingers rude
Shatter your leaves before the mellowing year.

The vehicle concerns the picking of berries prematurely from the trees. The tenor has to do with the poet's writing before he considers himself fully mature. Since laurel, myrtle, and ivy are traditionally associated with the poet, their choice in the vehicle suggests that the tenor is actually about poetic inspiration.

Tercet A three-line stanza, used with variations. It can stand as an independent unit, rhyming *aaa*, as Robert Frost does frequently in short one-stanza lyrics, or *aba*, as Browning does in "The Statue and the Bust." The tercet is also used with an interlocking rhyme scheme.

Threnody A lyric lamentation, written as an expression of grief upon the death of someone whom the poet loves or admires. Ralph Waldo Emerson's "Threnody" is a personal poem written upon the death of his son; Walt Whitman's "When Lilacs Last in the Dooryard Bloom'd" mourns the death of Abraham Lincoln.

Tragedy The concept of tragedy is not limited to drama; it is a serious way of looking at life. But, despite its dark side, tragedy is optimistic. It shows man in his moments of greatest adversity, but also reveals his fullest capacity to endure. His spirit is not easily broken. Tragedy testifies to man's dignity even when the odds are weighed heavily against him.

Because the term *tragedy* is often loosely used to refer to any disastrous event, it is well to consider what elements characterize it, particularly as it is used in literature. True tragedy, despite its variations throughout the history of literature, always seems to involve three main factors:

1. *An inevitable force.* In tragedy, man cannot escape the force of destiny. In ancient dramas, the element of necessity is almost always one beyond man's control. One can describe it in different ways as fate, the will of the gods, the force of the moral universe, or predestination, but whatever form it assumes man finds himself in conflict with a fixed and noncontrovertible force. Because death is the most unyielding fact of man's experience, tragedies usually concern themselves with men facing the hour of death.

Modern writers, however, less concerned with man's relation with metaphysical forces, have tended to write tragedies of living rather than tragedies of dying, to show man in relation to different kinds of shaping forces: his heredity, his environment, his own psychic nature, society in general. Because some of these have less inevitable influence on man and, unlike the universal will, cannot be conceived of as good, modern writers are sometimes said to have a diminished sense of the tragic. Whether diminished or not, the basic conflicts are different, and our reactions to the circumstances are therefore different. Existing conditions are seldom altered in a tragedy: the gods prevail, fate is accomplished, the harmony of the universe is restored, heredity is inescapable, society works its way. But if one believes that the gods are just, then good prevails, and man loses in the struggle. Seldom, however, do writers reveal society or environment as good. If man is a victim of environmental forces, no universal harmony prevails. Only evil conditions persist. The basic conflict in most general terms—and conflict is central to the tragic effect—is therefore between good and evil. In an ancient tragedy like *Oedipus*, the flaw in man leads him to upset the moral order. In a modern tragedy like Ibsen's *The Enemy of the People*, the flaw is in society; the individual is often seen as justified. This shifting view of the deterministic force is therefore one of the important differences in reading modern tragedy as opposed to classical tragedy.

2. *A protagonist with whom we can identify.* The protagonist of tragedy is commonly called the tragic hero. In ancient and Renaissance tragedies, he was inevitably a man of elevated station in life, but Aristotle had established that the hero should not be completely blameless. He is usually shown to be responsible for the consequences that fall to him. By some error or flaw in his

nature, he himself sets into motion a chain of circumstances which must work themselves inevitably to their end. If man only curses his fate and dies, if he does not have the integrity and strength to struggle, then tragedy cannot work its effects. Tragedy, therefore, deals with a change in man's fortune from good to bad. But the turn in fortune's wheel is only a change of outward circumstance. Tragedy concerns itself with conflict and changes in the inner man —the way in which he meets his fate, the way in which he struggles against it.

Modern tragedies, less concerned with the fate of kings and warriors, have introduced unheroic heroes and heroines like Willy in Arthur Miller's *Death of a Salesman* and Maurya, the mother in Synge's *Riders to the Sea,* not necessarily less heroic in spirit but less elevated in station. Their fall may be less catastrophic but not less meaningful in the total scheme of things. In fact, our own capacity to identify with them may be greater because of their lower status. Rich man or poor, king or peasant, man is capable of revealing tragic conflict.

3. *Tragic conflict and the outcome.* Tragic conflict is basically any struggle of man's will against some fate from which he cannot escape. The situation can vary from Antigone's determination to bury the body of her dead brother in defiance of the law of the state to Job's insistence on his own righteousness before God. Man is put to the test; man suffers. Tragedy reveals man in his weakness and in his strength. From the experience, he learns. He matures, he gains in wisdom, he sees more clearly his place in the scheme of things. His downfall and death may be his triumph. Tragedy brings about realizations of different kinds: that man is not totally self-sufficient, that man is vulnerable, that human existence is precarious, that man's spirit is indomitable, that man suffers retribution for his pride, that goodness prevails, that man will survive despite all odds. The experience of tragedy through literature keeps each man's life from being tragic. Tragedy inspires both pity and fear—pity for the sufferer and, by identification, fear for ourselves. Aristotle described this human response to tragedy as a catharsis, leaving us calmer and wiser for having emotionally experienced the conflict and destiny of a man less fortunate than we.

Tragic flaw or hamartia A concept derived from the *Poetics* where Aristotle describes the tragic hero as a person not entirely blameless or completely despicable but as a worthy man or woman whose character is marked by some flaw, which is ultimately responsible for his downfall. The flaw commonly depicted in Greek tragedy is *hubris* or *hybris,* a sense of overweening pride which causes man to think himself the equal of the gods. The "flaw" may also be interpreted as an error in judgment which results in direful consequences disproportionate to the act itself.

Tragicomedy The term *tragicomedy* arose as a critical expedient during the time when tragedy and comedy were rigidly defined. From the classical period through the Renaissance, tragedy was supposed to deal with the affairs of noble men; comedy with men of lesser breed. Tragedy ended in death; comedy in joyful resolution of circumstances. Tragicomedy was particularly useful to describe plays about noblemen whose destiny seemed to lead them to disaster but whose fortunes were happily transformed at the end. Shakespeare's *The Winter's Tale* fits the classification, as do many of the dramas written by Francis Beaumont and John Fletcher in the seventeenth century.

Trope A rhetorical figure of speech in which the literal meaning of words is altered in some way to convey a new or added meaning. Metaphor and simile are common tropes, although any variation of irony, hyperbole, understatement, ambiguity, or paradox falls into this classification.

In a more specialized sense, trope has reference to the elaborations on the liturgy which were permitted in medieval churches. The early ones were antiphonal variations by the choir or exchanges between a soloist and the chorus. *Quem quaeritis in sepulchro, o christicolae* (whom seek ye in the tomb, O followers of Christ?), the words of the angel to the three Marys, inserted into the Easter mass, possibly dating from the ninth century, is usually cited as the trope marking the revival of drama in Western Europe, for medieval morality and mystery plays were a direct outgrowth of these church presentations.

Ubi sunt A Latin phrase meaning "where are they?" It is often used as an opening line or a refrain of a poem. A question of this kind is a lament for the passing of fame, beauty, youth, or life itself. Each stanza of François Villon's "The Ballad of Dead Ladies," as translated by Dante Gabriel Rossetti, ends with the query: "But where are the snows of yesteryear?" The theme is the evanescence of beauty.

Ur A German prefix meaning "original," used as in *Urfaust* or *Ur-Hamlet* to refer to early versions or sources of more famous works or as in *Ursprache*, a hypothetical reconstruction of a primitive language.

Utopia Derived from two Greek words meaning "no place" and punning on two other Greek words meaning "good place." The "nowhere" of the literary utopia is the vision of an ideal world or state held by the writer. The utopia may be set forth in direct terms, as it is in Plato's *Republic* and Sir Thomas More's *Utopia* (1516) or it may be described satirically in terms of the opposite of what is ideal, as in George Orwell's *1984* and Aldous Huxley's *Brave New World*.

Vehicle   *See* **Tenor.**

Versification   When words are combined with one another, a rhythmic effect is inevitable, simply because words themselves have accented and unaccented syllables. Any combination of words sets up a rising and falling movement. If the movement is regular and repeated, it is called meter. Meter is measured rhythm. The metrical form of a group of words is the chief distinction between prose and verse. Both are rhythmical, but verse is frequently written in a set pattern. Even though twentieth-century poets have veered away from strictly measured verse to freer rhythmic patterns, many poems may still be marked by means of traditional units. The measurement of a line in terms of accents is called scansion. (*See* **Free verse.**)

Scansion

The basic measuring unit of verse is a foot. In the English language, a foot consists of one stressed syllable and one or more unstressed syllables in a particular arrangement producing a definable meter. This is a scansion based on accents. In accenting, we use both stress and pitch to highlight certain sounds. Other languages base meters on long and short sounds, but accent is a more suitable system for English.

Traditional scansion makes no distinction between degrees of stress. Theoretically, all stressed syllables are of equal length. Unstressed syllables are also theoretically equal. Thus the marking system is reduced to two symbols: ′ for a stressed syllable, ⌣ for an unstressed one.

The common metric feet of English verse are four:

1. iambus, producing iambic meter, consisting of an unstressed syllable followed by a stressed one:
    before, delight, inspire, serene
2. trochee, producing trochaic meter, consisting of a stressed syllable followed by an unstressed one:
    after, picture, gather, recent
3. anapest, producing anapestic meter, consisting of two unstressed syllables followed by a stressed syllable:
    underneath, Lebanese, entertain, indirect

4. dactyl, producing dactylic meter, consisting of one stressed
   syllable followed by two unstressed ones:

   ′ ∪ ∪ ′ ∪ ∪ ′ ∪ ∪ ′ ∪ ∪
   equally, iciness, obligate, glamorous

The other possible combinations of stress and lack of stress are
used primarily as substitute feet in order to vary the rhythm of
regular metric lines:

1. spondee, consisting of two stressed syllables:

   ′ ′ ′ ′
   hymn book, lifeboat
2. pyrrhic, consisting of two unaccented syllables:

   ∪ ′/ ∪ ′/ ∪ ∪
   the supernatural
3. amphibrach, consisting of an unaccented syllable, an accented,
   and another unaccented one in that order.

   ∪ ′ ∪ ∪ ′ ∪
   however, elation

Other variations, of course, are possible. For example, an anapest can substitue for an iambic foot or a dactyl for a trochaic
foot; or, in the first foot of an iambic line, a trochee or a spondee
is commonly substituted for the regular foot:

′ ∪/ ∪ ′ / ∪ ′/ ∪ ′ / ∪ ′
Fair is my love, and cruel as she's fair.

—Samuel Daniel, *Delia*, VI

′ ′/ ∪ ′ / ∪ ′ / ∪ ′/ ∪ ′
Look Delia, how we 'steem the half-blown rose

—Daniel, *Delia*, XXI

The second line from *Delia* XXI illustrates the tendency sometimes for the poet to truncate a word (*esteem* to *'steem*) in order
to keep a regular meter. This may also be done by elision:

∪ ′/∪′/∪ ′ / ∪ ′/∪ ′
Thus policy in love, t'anticipate
∪ ′/ ∪ ′ / ∪ ′ / ∪ ′ / ∪ ′
The ills that were not, grew to faults assured.

—Shakespeare, "Sonnet 118"

Or by giving value to a syllable that is usually unpronounced:

∪ ′ / ∪ ′ /∪ ′/∪ ′ /∪ ′
O Prince, O Chief of many thronéd Powers

—Milton, *Paradise Lost*, I, 128

Lines of verse sometimes end with an extra unstressed syllable,
called a weak or feminine ending:

∪ ′ / ∪ ′ / ∪ ′/∪ ′/ ∪ ′/∪
A thing of beauty is a joy forever

—Keats, "Endymion"

If the final extra syllable is stressed, it is called a masculine ending, which may occur when the final foot of a trochaic line is incomplete:

／ ∪／ ／ ∪／ ／ ∪／ ／
Russet lawns and fallows grey,
／ ∪／ ／ ∪／ ／
Where the nibbling flocks do stray;

—Milton, "L'Allegro"

At times, the regular running meter of a line can be sustained, yet natural speech intonations will impose a different accentual pattern upon the line, resulting in a kind of counterpoint:

／ ／ ／ ／ ／ ∪／ ／ ∪ ／／ ／ ／ (speech emphasis)
∪ ／ ／ ∪ ／／∪／ ／ ∪ ／／ ∪ ／ (running meter)
Wilt thou then antedate some new made vow?

∪ ／ ∪ ／
Or say that now
／ ∪／ ／ ／／ ／ ／／ ∪   ／ ／∪ ／ (speech emphasis)
∪ ／ ／∪ ／／ ∪ ／／ ∪   ／ ／∪ ／ (running meter)
We are not just those persons, which we were?

—Donne, "Woman's Constancy"

Common Meters

The versification of a poem is described in terms of its predominant meter and the length of its line determined by the number of feet. The counting system of prosody is monometer (1), dimeter (2), trimeter (3), tetrameter (4), pentameter (5), hexameter (6), heptameter (7), octometer (8). The meter of a poem therefore may be identified as iambic pentameter, trochaic trimeter, dactylic hexameter, or various other combinations.

iambic monometer

A line consisting of a single foot is frequently used in combination with longer lines for a special effect:

∪ ／／ ∪ ∪ ／ ／ ∪ ／∪
And last, till you write your letter,

∪ ／
Yet she
∪ ／
Will be
／ ∪／∪ ／ ／∪ ／ /∪ ／
False, ere I come, to two or three.

—Donne, "Go and Catch a Falling Star"

iambic dimeter and trimeter

∪ ／/∪ ／
Bianca, let
∪ ／ ∪ ／
Me pay the debt
∪ ／ ／ ∪ ／／ ∪ ／
I owe thee for a kiss
∪ ／ ／ ∪ ／
Thou lend'st to me,

⏑ ′ /⏑ ′
And I to thee
⏑   ′ /⏑ ′ /⏑ ′
Will render ten for this:

—Herrick, "Kissing Usury"

iambic tetrameter

⏑   ′ /⏑   ′/⏑ ′ /⏑ ′
Those cherries fairly do enclose
⏑   ′/⏑ ′ / ⏑ ′/⏑ ′
Of orient pearl a double row;
⏑   ′ / ⏑ ′ /⏑ ′ /⏑ ′
Which when her lovely laughter shows,
⏑   ′ / ⏑ ′ ⏑ ′ / ⏑ ′
They look like rosebuds filled with snow.

—Campion, "There Is a Garden in Her Face"

iambic pentameter

When iambic pentameter is used for epic poetry in English, it
is called heroic verse:

⏑ ′ / ⏑ ′/ ⏑ ′ /⏑ ′ / ⏑ ′
Of Man's first disobedience, and the fruit
⏑ ′/ ⏑ ′ /⏑ ′ ⏑   ′ /⏑ ′
Of that forbidden tree, whose mortal taste
⏑   ′ /⏑ ′/ ⏑   ′ / ⏑ ′/ ⏑ ′
Brought death into the world, and all our woe,
⏑   ′/ ⏑ ′/⏑ ′ /⏑ ′ /⏑′ Man
With loss of Eden, till one greater Man
⏑ ′ /⏑ ′ / ⏑ ′ /⏑ ′ ⏑ ′
Restore us, and regain the blissful seat,
′   ′ / ⏑ ′
Sing, Heavenly Muse . . .

—Milton, *Paradise Lost*

When verse is written in rhyming lines of iambic pentameter, the
form is called the heroic couplet:

⏑   ′ / ⏑   ′ / ⏑   ′ / ⏑ ′ / ⏑ ′
Some truth there was, but dashed and brewed with lies,
⏑   ′ / ⏑   ′ / ⏑ ′/⏑ ′ ⏑ ′
To please the fools, and puzzle all the wise:
⏑ ′ /⏑ ′ / ⏑ ′ /⏑ ′/⏑ ′
Succeeding times did equal folly call,
⏑ ′/ ⏑ ′/ ⏑ ′ /⏑ ′/⏑ ′
Believing nothing, or believing all.

—Dryden, "Absalom and Achitophel"

When poetry is written in unrhymed iambic pentameter, the form
is called blank verse:

′   ⏑/ ⏑ ′/ ⏑ ′/ ⏑ ′ /⏑ ′
Something there is that doesn't love a wall,
⏑   ′ / ⏑ ′ /⏑ ′ / ⏑ ′/⏑ ′
That sends the frozen-ground-swell under it,
⏑   ′ / ⏑ ′ /⏑ ′ / ⏑ ′/⏑ ′
And spills the upper boulders in the sun;
⏑   ′ / ′ ′ /⏑ ′/ ⏑ ′ /⏑ ′
And makes gaps even two can pass abreast.

—Frost, "Mending Wall"

iambic hexameter or Alexandrine

And streams of purple blood new dies the verdant fields.
>   —Spenser, *The Faerie Queene*

trochaic tetrameter

Up, lad, up, 'tis late for lying:
  Hear the drums of morning play;
>   —Housman, "Reveille"

A line which lacks part of its last foot is called catalectic.

trochaic octometer

Many a night from yonder ivied casement, ere I went to rest,
Did I look on great Orion sloping slowly to the West.
>   —Tennyson, "Locksley Hall"

anapestic tetrameter

And the widows of Asshur are loud in their wail,
And the idols are broke in the temple of Baal;
>   —Byron, "The Destruction of Sennacherib"

anapestic hexameter

Of the maiden thy mother men sing as a goddess with grace clad around;
Thou art throned where another was king; where another was queen
    she is crowned.
>   —Swinburne, "Hymn to Proserpine"

dactylic dimeter

Cannon to right of them,
Cannon to left of them,
Cannon in front of them
  Volley'd and thunder'd;
>   —Tennyson, "The Charge of the Light Brigade"

dactylic hexameter

Over two shadowless waters, adrift as a pinnace in peril
>   —Swinburne, "Evening on the Broads"

Caesura

The caesura of a line is the natural pause that results from the grammar or logic of the words. The caesura commonly occurs after the fourth, fifth, or sixth syllable in a ten-syllable line, but it is by no means limited to those junctures. If the caesura occurs after a stressed syllable, it is called masculine; if it occurs after an unstressed syllable, it is called feminine:

Of all this servile herd || the worst is he   (masculine)

That in proud dullness || joins with quality,   (feminine)

—Pope, *An Essay on Criticism*

Poets often shift the caesura in successive lines to discourage a metronomic reading of their lines.

Villanelle   A poem of nineteen lines, consisting of five tercets rhyming *aba,* ending with a quatrain rhyming *abaa,* and featuring the repetition of lines in a set pattern. The first and third lines of the first tercet, here indicated as A^1 and A^2, are repeated alternately in their entirety throughout the remaining stanzas in the following manner: A^1bA^2, abA^1; abA^2, abA^1, abA^2, aba^1A^2. Dylan Thomas' "Do Not Go Gentle into That Good Night" is a well-known example. Theodore Roethke's "The Waking" is a villanelle with slight variations in the repeated lines.

Wit   The current implications of the word *wit* have their source in a variety of meanings attributed to the word throughout its long history. The present conception of wit as an intellectual brand of humor retains a remnant of its oldest meanings as "knowledge" or "the seat of knowledge," derived from the Anglo-Saxon *witan,* meaning "to know." Its present association with swift perception and cleverness bears something in common with the seventeenth-century use of the term to designate the "fancy" or "creative imagination"—the power of conceiving. Its modern implication of aptness, even patness, has something in common with its eighteenth-century use as the exercise of judgment, resulting in propriety and good sense. In most ages, the word has been linked with verbal ingenuity, quickness, and conciseness— the products of a bright mind—but mainly since the eighteenth century it has taken on an implication of laughableness. *See* **Epigram.**

Zeugma   A rhetorical trope (q.v.), usually of a humorous nature, producing a shift in verbal context by having one part of speech, usually a preposition or a verb, function with two subjects or two objects, which are in themselves disproportionate:

> Hear thou, great Anna! whom three realms obey,
> Dost sometimes counsel take—and sometimes tea.
>
> —Pope, "The Rape of the Lock"

Index